Translation Practices Explained

Translation Practices Explained is a series of coursebooks designed to help self-learners and teachers of translation.

Each volume focuses on a specific type of translation, in most cases corresponding to actual courses available in translator-training institutions. Special volumes are devoted to professional areas where labour-market demands are growing: court interpreting, community interpreting, European-Union texts, multimedia translation, text revision, electronic tools, and software and website localization.

The authors are practising translators or translator trainers in the fields concerned. Although specialists, they explain their professional insights in a manner accessible to the wider learning public.

Designed to complement the *Translation Theories Explained* series, these books start from the recognition that professional translation practices require something more than elaborate abstraction or fixed methodologies. The coursebooks are located close to work on authentic texts, simulating but not replacing the teacher's hands-on role in class. Self-learners and teachers are encouraged to proceed inductively, solving problems as they arise from examples and case studies. The series thus offers a body of practical information that can orient and complement the learning process.

Each volume includes activities and exercises designed to help self-learners consolidate their knowledge and to encourage teachers to think creatively about their classes. Updated reading lists and website addresses will also help individual learners gain further insight into the realities of professional practice.

Anthony Pym
Series Editor

Translating Official Documents

Roberto Mayoral Asensio

ST JEROME
PUBLISHING

St. Jerome Publishing
Manchester, UK & Northampton, MA

Published by
   St. Jerome Publishing
   2 Maple Road West, Brooklands
   Manchester, M23 9HH, United Kingdom
   Tel +44 161 973 9856
   Fax +44 161 905 3498
   stjerome@compuserve.com
   http://www.stjerome.co.uk

ISBN 1-900650-65-7 (pbk)
ISSN 1470-966X (*Translation Practices Explained*)

Printed and bound in Great Britain by
Alden Group Ltd, Osney Mead, Oxford, UK

Cover design by
Steve Fieldhouse, Oldham, UK (+44 161 620 2263)

Typeset by
Delta Typesetters, Cairo, Egypt
Email: hilali1945@hotmail.com

British Library Cataloguing in Publication Data
A catalogue record of this book is available from the British Library

Library of Congress Cataloging-in-Publication Data
Mayoral Asensio, Roberto, 1950-
  Translating official documents / Roberto Mayoral Asensio.
      p. cm. -- (Translation practices explained)
Includes bibliographical references and index.
  ISBN 1-900650-65-7 (pbk. : alk. paper)
 1. Translating and interpreting--Study and teaching. 2.
Documentation--Translating. I. Title. II. Series.
  P306.97.D62M39 2003
  418'.02'071--dc21
                                                    2002156719

Contents

Acknowledgements

The following colleagues, among others, have contributed their advice, knowledge, expertise, time and friendship to this work. They prove that it can still be said that the translator's profession is characterized by solidarity, collaboration and generosity. Quite often their opinions differ from the author's.

Flavia Caciagli, Italy
Bart De Rooze, Belgium
Fee Engemann, Germany
Manuel Feria García, Spain
Nancy Festinger, US
Celia Filipetto, Catalonia, Spain
Natividad Gallardo San Salvador, Spain
Rafael Gil Esteban, Spain
Miguel Ángel González Reyes, Spain
Dennis McKenna, US
Montserrat Oriol, United Kingdom
Anthony Pym, Catalonia, Spain
Sally Robinson, Australia
Nicholas Smith, United Kingdom
Josep Peñarroja Fa, Catalonia, Spain
Catherine Way, Spain

Dedication

To
Natividad Gallardo, Dorothy Kelly, Cathy Way, Ada Franzoni de Moldavski, Rafael Gil, Josep Peñarroja, Celia Filipetto, Manuel Feria, Anabel Borja, Marian Labrum, Enrique Alcaraz and Anthony Pym

To
Colegio de Traductores Públicos de la Ciudad de Buenos Aires, Argentina
Associació de Traductors i Intèrprets Jurats de Catalunya, Spain

To
the Pakistani community in Spain
all my students

1. Introduction

This book is about official written translation and official translators in the world. Official translations may be broadly defined as *translations that meet the requirements to serve as legally valid instruments in a target country*. This kind of translation is of growing importance in the increasingly smaller world we live in. It arouses interest in students, scholars, trainers and practitioners. Given the absence of any comprehensive monograph on this subject, our study is more than justified.

However, our task is not easy. Official translation takes on extremely varied forms throughout the world, and discussing the practice of translation is always difficult when you must exclude references to a specific pair of languages in order to reach a wider audience. In order to overcome this problem, English will be the source text in our examples and, for the target language, I will give an English version of what would have been my translation. Since translation procedures are simply expression procedures, my point is that the transition from the source to the target can be explained through intralinguistic operations. Hopefully, re-expression in the same language may be an accurate enough representation of many of the translation procedures that occur between two different languages.

When considering the social context of this kind of translation, I will make frequent references to the Spanish situation. My intention is to use them as an example, not to present the Spanish situation as ideal or unique.

The discussion of official translation in this work is meant to portray only its practice and not theoretical considerations. This has proved an impossible task; even when priority has been given to introducing the reader to practice, generalizations about practice always lead us to theoretical considerations. Teaching practice consists not only of explaining how to translate a text; it necessarily implies endowing future translators with critical tools that will allow them to make their own choices consciously and creatively.

Official translation is not a well-defined activity. It overlaps with fields such as oral translation, legal translation, court translating and interpreting, and community interpreting. Nevertheless, I have tried to restrict the description to the most common types of translation tasks we may find.

Official translation is often considered an activity subject to numerous strict norms, or as an extremely constrained form of translation. However, this is not always the case. Firstly, there are many different kinds of norms, and their degree of obligation varies from legal norms to uses and customs. Secondly, the number of compulsory norms in our field is usually extremely low. Thirdly, transgression of the norms is inherent to the practice of any kind of translation, as this is the only way to develop new techniques and reach higher standards of quality. Lastly, even the most constrained ways of translating admit a high degree of freedom and creativity, which allows translators to find their job extremely enjoyable.

Work as an official translator makes you feel socially useful, even powerful; it gives you a prominence that other kinds of translation do not. Official translation is also one of the most personalized types of translation. It lets you meet your client and the recipient of your work. Official translation is strongly linked to ethical considerations. Being an official translator brings to life the idea of being a bridge between cultures, for which the client's trust is an indispensable condition. Official translation also allows high doses of creativity. It is a prestigious profession and a very old activity: official translation in Spain has been documented as far back as the ninth century; the first reference to 'sworn translation' was in 1551 (Feria 2002a).

Welcome to a whole new world.

2. Professional Practice

In Spain, the official written translating of documents is called *sworn transla-tion* and is carried out by professionals called *sworn translators*. But official documents are also rendered by translators who are non-professional or have not achieved sworn translator status. We will thus call the translating of these documents *official translation*, rather than *sworn translation*. When we refer to translators who perform official translation, we will call them *official transla-tors*, whatever their professional condition may be.

Documents may be translated for different purposes. They may be intended for the government of a country or community speaking a foreign language, often in order to certify allegations in a legal or administrative process and usu-ally as evidence in a court case. They may be translated so that a legal situation originating in a foreign language country can be recognized, or in order to ap-ply for the recognition or validation of merits acquired in a foreign country. Legal texts can also be translated in order to apply the source norm to foreign citizens, which is a basic principle of Private International Law. For instance, a Moroccan citizen living in Spain can require their divorce demand to follow Moroccan law; in that case, the Spanish judge and lawyers may need a transla-tion of the corresponding law, jurisprudence and doctrine plus the official translator's expert commentary.

Since official translations must include a statement that certifies fidelity to the source text, the translator becomes a *public authenticator* of the contents of the translation. In order to acquire the status of an authenticator, a translator must sit an exam set by the Spanish Ministry of Foreign Affairs. Translators with a university degree in translation and interpreting must have met certain requirements in order to receive the appointment without taking the exam. These conditions are specific to Spain and situations vary enormously all around the world, as we will discuss later.

Documents for official translation may contain any of the following elements:

❑ Recorded elements: births, marriages, academic studies, deaths, wills, ille-gal activities, or other legal or administrative acts (such as sales agreements or medical prescriptions)
❑ Documentary elements, such as letters, reports, blank certification forms, completed certification forms, validated certifications, translations, author-ized translations and authorized and validated translations
❑ Validating elements, such as the certification of formalities corresponding to different moments of a proceeding (the certifications of a registrar, a notary public, a court clerk, the Hague apostille, for example)

The *purpose* of the translation – the *Skopos* named by the functionalist school (cf. Nord 1997) – would seem to be enviably well defined for official translation if compared to other translation situations. It should be fairly easy for the translator to find the adequate way to perform their communicative act, remaining faithful to the original text and loyal to the demands of the final receiver.

The official *translator's* profile would also seem well defined. The translator is a person who complies with the requirements established by local legislation (the Ministry of Foreign Affairs in Spain, although there are no requirements in countries such as Ireland). They should be competent in the fields of economic and legal translation, and they must consciously assume responsibility for all the consequences and liabilities of their function as public authenticator.

The *receiver's* profile is perfectly defined as well: it is the courts or other branches of the public administration, usually under the ministries of education, the interior (police), foreign affairs, and so on who receive the translation.

The *texts to be translated* are documents that must function in a linguistic and cultural community different to the one in which they originated. If we are to follow the lead of the examinations for joining the profession or the requirements, these texts are in the economic and legal fields. But the slightest incursion into professional practice shows that any text is liable to be the object of official translation if it falls within a judicial process or a request of acknowledgement of rights before any kind of administrative body (see Section 4.1, Types).

The language *from which one translates* is the one that the official translator is entitled to work from. Later we will discuss the way in which a narrow application of this principle would render certain documents impossible to translate.

2.1 Professional practice around the world

If we search for a 'norm' describing the way official translation is conducted around the world, we will not find it; the reality is too rich and varied. The models or prototypes that we come across are diverse and do not fit exactly in any scheme. There are countries with absolute regulation of both the activity and professional practice (Argentina); countries where entry to the profession is regulated but not the practice itself (Spain); and others where neither of them is regulated (Cuba, Russia). In some countries only the practice in the courts is regulated (Italy); in others the activity is regulated both within and outside of the courts (Denmark). Sometimes written translation functions almost as an appendix to oral translation (United States); elsewhere written translation is given at least the same importance (Spain). In some countries, translating into a non-mother tongue is considered improper practice (United Kingdom); in others (Spain, Italy), working in both directions is accepted (from and into the translator's mother tongue). There may be mandatory membership of an association (we will call them *professional societies*) (Argentina); there may be only non-official voluntary membership of what we will call *professional associations*, especially created for official translators (Catalonia[1]); or there may be no special association at all beyond a general professional one for all kinds of translators (although France, for example, has two associations: one for literary, the other for the rest). Translators for the courts are sometimes considered a type of judicial expert, as is the case in Mexico and France, but this is far from the case elsewhere.

Unfortunately the task of describing this variety in detail goes beyond the possibilities of our work. Having consulted the Committee of the International Federation of Translators responsible for this kind of translation, I was told that they were not able to provide a list of professional associations dealing with court interpreting: "there are just too many, and sometimes they have only local membership". However, Ms Mevrou W. J. G. Heres, from the Netherlands, is currently conducting a study of the situation of the profession in Europe.

In what follows, we have attempted to systematize the various descriptions of official translation. The result is necessarily inaccurate and simplistic, since the information available for each specific case varies. Countries such as the United States or Germany, for example, offer such a rich and diverse situation that they resist systematization.

2.2. Features of official translation in different countries and regions

Name for the translator

The many names used around the world for official translators include the following:

traductor público (public translator, Argentina); *tradutor publico e intérprete comercial* (public translator and commercial interpreter, Brazil); *traductor/intèrpret jurat* (sworn translator/interpreter, Catalonia); non-existent (Cuba); *statsautoriseret translatør* (translator authorized by the State, Denmark); *traducteur juré* (sworn translator, France, name not legally valid); *traducteur assermenté* (sworn translator, France, name no longer used); *traducteur expert judiciaire* (judicial expert

---

[1] Here and throughout we will refer to Catalonia, Galicia and the Basque Country without adding the necessary information that these are regions of Spain. Since each of these regions has its own language and laws governing official translation, they constitute independent spaces for the purposes of our survey.

translator, France); *traductor e intérprete xurado* (sworn translator and interpreter, Galicia); *ermächtigter Übersetzer* (authorized translator, Germany); *beidigter Überstzer* (sworn translator, Germany); *traductor jurado* (sworn translator, Guatemala); *esküdt fordító* (sworn translator, Hungary); (non-existent, Ireland); *traduttore giurato/consulenti tecnici/perito* (sworn translator/expert, Italy); *perito traductor, traductor certificado* (translating expert, certified translator, Mexico); *traducteur agréé* (certified translator, Morocco); *traductor público juramentado* (sworn public translator, Peru); *tlumacz przysiegly* (sworn translator, Poland); (Russia, non-existent); *intérprete jurado* (sworn interpreter, Spain); (UK non-existent), *scrivener notary* (UK); *traductor público* (public translator, Uruguay); *certified interpreter/ ATA-accredited translator* (US); *intérprete público* (public interpreter, Venezuela).

Authorized activities

The things that official translators are authorized to do also vary considerably:
Official translators can only do written translation: Catalonia, Germany, United Kingdom.
Official translators can also do oral translation: Argentina, Brazil, Denmark, Galicia, Italy; Luxembourg, Poland, Spain, Venezuela.
Official translators are included under the more general category of judicial experts: France, Italy, Mexico.
Official interpreters may also work in written translation: Germany, US.
Courts may appoint unofficial translators for particular situations: Germany, Italy, Mexico, Spain.
Official translators are the only ones entitled to translate official documents: Denmark, Poland.

Direction (into mother tongue/into non-mother tongue)

Both directions: Argentina; Denmark; Italy; Spain (currently); Uruguay; US; Venezuela.
Only into mother tongue: Peru; Mexico; Spain (prior to 1996).

Regulation of the profession

Official translation is regulated by law: Argentina; Brazil; Catalonia (partially); Galicia (partially); Denmark; Germany; Morocco; Peru; Spain (partially).
Only translation for the courts is regulated: France; Germany (also for notaries); Italy; Mexico.
Only interpreting for the Courts is regulated: US.

Jurisdiction

National level: Brazil; Denmark; Mexico; Poland; Spain.
Regional level: Argentina (province); Germany (*Land*); US (state).
Exclusively for one court: France; Morocco.

Swearing-in ceremony

Brazil; Germany; Italy; Luxembourg; Mexico; Morocco.

Specific examination

Brazil; Catalonia; Galicia; Guatemala; Morocco (*stage*); Poland; Spain; US; Venezuela.

Authorizing body

Judicial authorities: Germany; Poland; US (for interpreters).
Ministry of Foreign Affairs or consulates: Germany; Peru; Spain.
Ministry of Justice or equivalent: Germany; Italy; Luxembourg; Mexico; Morocco.
Ministry of Commerce: Brazil (*Juntas Comerciales*); Mexico.
Ministry of Education or equivalent: Argentina; Galicia; US; Uruguay.
Ministry of Culture: Catalonia.
Notaries: Russia.
General translation degrees: Catalonia; Denmark; Galicia; Italy; Morocco; Spain.
Foreign-language degrees: Poland; Russia.
Professional associations: Institute of Translation and Interpreting, Institute of Linguists (UK), NAJIT, ATA (US).

Authenticating authority

Professional Society (Argentina); *Juntas Comerciales* (Ministry of Labour, Industry and Commerce) (Brazil); Department of Culture/General Directorate of Linguistic Policy (Catalonia); General Directorate of Mercantile Societies (Denmark); Department of Education, General Directorate of Linguistic Policy (Galicia); Ministry of Justice (Italy); notary public (Mexico); consulates/town council (Morocco); notary public (Russia); Ministry of Foreign Affairs/Local Delegations of Central Government (Spain); Notary public/Ministry of Foreign Affairs/Consulate (United Kingdom).

Associations

Professional Societies:
Argentina (City of Buenos Aires, Province of Córdoba, Province of Catamarca, Province of Santa Fe); Uruguay; Venezuela.

General professional associations for translators:
Argentina; Australia; Austria; Basque Country; Belgium; Brazil; Bulgaria; Canada; Chile; China; Cyprus; Czech Republic; Denmark; Finland; France; Galicia; Germany; Greece; Guatemala; Holland; Hungary; Indonesia; International Federation of Translators (FIT); Iraq; Ireland; Israel; Italy; Japan; Jordan; Mexico; New Zealand; Nigeria; Norway; Panama; Poland; Portugal; Russia; Slovakia; South Africa; South Korea; Sri Lanka; Sweden; Switzerland; Syria; United Kingdom; US; Yugoslavia.

Specific professional associations for official translators:
Balearic Islands, Spain; Basque Country; Brazil; Catalonia; Denmark; France; Greece; Committee for Court Interpreting and Legal Translation, FIT; Morocco; Norway; Poland; Quebec, Canada; Sweden; US; Valencia, Spain.

Suggested activities

1) Define the situation of official translation in your country: legal norms, practice, attestation formulas, validation of the official translation, associations and fees.
2) Assess this situation. Which aspects do you consider could be improved?
3) Visit the FIT Website. Search for any information useful to an official translator.

3. The Social Context

3.1 Participants

Parties involved in the document

In accordance with the terms used by professionals in this field, here we will refer to a *document* when other branches of translation studies would refer to a *text*. Basically we can find two different situations involving official documents:

1. The document reflects facts about the legal subject or subjects (birth certificate, marriage certificate, academic transcript). In legal and administrative practice, these subjects are called the *party* or *parties involved*, or *the interested party*. The particular interpretation of the document rendered by the translator may either benefit or damage the interested party. Further, in a sense, it also may benefit or damage the public authorities, if we consider the interested party and the authorities as having opposed interests (validation of study courses, residence application or work permit).
2. The document reflects a legal relationship between *different parties*. These parties may hold conflicting interests (for instance, a contract). The particular interpretation of the document rendered by the translator may benefit one of the parties and damage the other.

Parties not mentioned in the document

In both of the above situations, the result of the translation may affect parties that are not mentioned in the document. These parties may benefit from or be damaged by the translator's rendition if, for example, a translation of an academic transcript biased in a way favourable to a certain candidate may harm other candidates for the same position.

The client (and/or their representatives)

The client is the person (or persons) who requests the translator to carry out a translation assignment and pays for it. Usually the client and the involved party are one and the same. It may also be the case that the client is the involved party's *attorney* or *representative* – at law or in fact – and it may also occur that the client identifies with one of the *parties* of a lawsuit, or even the *judicial body* that is to settle the claim.

The recipient

The recipient is the administrative or judicial authority that is to acknowledge the validity of the translated document. Even though the courts are usually the administrative body that acts as the recipient of the documents, it is also common for other administrative institutions (Ministry of Education, universities or university departments, Social Security administration, etc.) to be so. More rarely, the recipient is not an official institution but a private entity. For instance, in Spain some translated documents are delivered to a bank (La Caixa) when applying for its scholarships.

The translator

In official translation, the translator is the person who translates and sometimes a person legally appointed to act as an *official* or *sworn translator*.

The terminology of Translation Studies

German-language *Skopostheorie* (cf. Nord 1997:19-22) considers translation as interpersonal action involving the following participants: translator, initiator, commissioner, addressee, and user. Unfortunately these terms are not easily applied to official translation, since the borderlines between them are not, in my opinion, well defined. Here we will use *recipient* instead of *addressee*.

The involved party and their representatives work, as a party, for a favourable interpretation of the document.

It is inherent to legal or administrative actions that the one who claims a title or right tries to achieve the most favourable interpretation of that right. The legal system thus assumes that the claiming party and their counsel must propose interpretations of the facts and the law that are favourable to their interests. Laws and regulations are deemed to be subject to interpretation and the parties and their attorneys are in charge of elaborating this interpretation. But a non-objective description of facts is not allowed; the mechanisms that control the objectivity of the presentation of facts are the administrative officers and all public authenticators.

The recipient (generally, the public authorities) as a damaged party

As a consequence of the above, the public authorities inevitably suspect that the parties will alter facts to their advantage. The authorities consequently behave as a party exposed to deception and fraud.

The translator, between the devil and the deep blue sea

Translators of official documents quite often find themselves involved in an extremely contradictory situation. On the one hand, the involved party is the commissioner of the translation and the one who pays; on the other, translators take on the role of a public authenticator and a protector from biased interpretations of facts. This situation is not only the privilege of the translator of official documents; it is shared by notaries public, although the attitude of the public authorities toward notaries is radically different from that shown toward official translators. All things considered, official translators should always fall back on their codes of ethics, and their translations should contain as objective a description of facts as possible. That is, they should attach more importance to their role as public authenticators than to their position as the client's payee.

In other cases (such as criminal cases), the translator is commissioned not by one of the involved parties but the public authority itself. This means the above dilemmas should be resolved, although the translator will still be subject to the authorities' general prejudices against translators.

Is the official translator's honesty to be presumed?

As is the case for anyone, the translator of official documents should be allowed the presumption of innocence; they should be presumed to be honest (objective in their translations). This does not mean that all official translators are always honest. There is always a bad apple around. Even in those cases when selective tests are necessary to obtain the appointment of official translator, those tests assess knowledge and skills, not morality or ethics.

Is the official translator's competence to be presumed?

In some cases, facts are rendered in a biased way due to the dishonesty of the translator, who is working for their client and not for the truth. But this is not always the case. Sometimes the change is due to the incompetence of the translator, who has misunderstood the original text or has not been able to express their understanding in an exact way. Selection procedures for official translators are usually stringent, but all of us are witnesses to translations that prove that the official translator does not always meet the high professional standards required by their appointment.

The interested party's attorneys and the translator

A brutal collision can occur between the attorney's culture and the translator's culture. A lawyer is supposed to present facts in the most favourable way for their client, whereas the official translator is supposed to present facts in an objective fashion. It has even been said that lawyers make bad official translators. As with all generalizations, this is unfair, but it reflects a feeling common enough among official translators.

3.2 Loyalties

When translating official documents, the final recipient (the judge, law enforcement officer, academic authority, company) is the one who imposes their
conditions on the translator. If we attend first to the demands or interests of the
client, the act of translation is likely to fail; the translation may not be accepted
by its final recipient. The client will stress the merits or circumstances favourable to the validation, credit, permission or hiring. The final recipient will do
their best to avoid being deceived, avoiding forgery; their demands for fidelity
and literalism will be very strong. The translator will show a strong inclination
to explain cultural and institutional differences that can be found in the original
text, since they know that when an equivalent is not found in literal and mor-
phological translation, you are supposed to search for that equivalent through
explicative, exegetic procedures. This inclination on the part of the translator
can meet with frontal opposition from the final recipient. The translator might
be forced to suppress it in order to fulfil the client's expectations. An intercultural
translator cannot imagine fidelity without an explanation; the recipient of the
translation cannot imagine fidelity without literalism; the client does not care
much about fidelity if their *validation* goals are achieved. The general suspicion of forgery causes the translator to be suspicious of their client and possibly
afraid of being punished for participating in an unlawful action. This usually
acts as an opposing force to the tendency to *interpret* the original; it will make
the translator bend to the demands of literalism more easily than when dealing
with other kinds of translation. Jurists think that the interpretation of a legal text
is only valid when this interpretation is either authentic – that is, it proceeds
from the legislator – or authorized – when it proceeds from doctrine and jurisprudence, as is the case with judges. Their claim for literalism is based on the
idea that legislators, doctrine and jurisprudence are the only sources entitled to
interpret the text. Their criteria for interpreting legal texts are based on the assump-
tion that interpretation will take place in the same territory in which the texts
were originally produced. A valid exception is, for them, the case of international
instruments, with two legislators, but they exclude the possibility of interpretation when the texts are supposed to have effect in a third country, when the
translator intervenes. For jurists, a translator must not interpret. Some judges
even dislike the name 'interpreters' for oral judicial translators (Mikkelson 2000).

Resistance to the final recipient's demands can lead to the translation being
declared void, so failing the client's interest. I am in favour of accepting the
final recipient's impositions when they are manifest or evident. The official
translator's main aim is not to keep their own conscience at peace as to the
translation procedures adopted. A translation that is perfect from an academic
or scholastic point of view could turn out to be a failure from a professional
point of view.

In my opinion, you thus cannot offer universal solutions for the translation of this kind of document. This is because the official translator is often simultaneously subject to different demands, often highly incompatible, such as fidelity, literalism, transparency, plausibility, identification, good style (clarity, fluency, adequate and coherent terminology and phraseology, etc.). In order to illustrate this, I shall explain a case in which I had to choose between fidelity to truth and the client's demands:

TRANSLATION CASE

A client gave me the following documents for their official translation:

1) an academic transcript from a United States *Community College*[1] certifying one academic year of an *Associate in Science*[2] degree with a major in Nursing
2) an academic transcript from a *university*[3] certifying two academic years and the award of the corresponding *Associate in Science in Technical Nursing* degree
3) the diploma corresponding to the *Associate in Science in Technical Nursing* degree
4) a certificate of professional registration to exercise as a *Registered Nurse*[4], including the client's license number
5) the corresponding apostilles and legalizations
6) the translation into Spanish of each of the above documents, which the client declared had been obtained from the Spanish Embassy in the United States.

The client aimed to use the translations to obtain accreditation corresponding to the Spanish degree of *Diplomado en Enfermería*, a three-year course of

---

[1] A *Community College* is a public college that offers the first two years of higher education and which grants *Associate* degrees but not *Bachelor* or higher degrees. Generally, its students live off-campus. It covers local needs and it is the equivalent to a *Junior College*. *College*, versus *University*, is a higher education institution that mainly offers a first four-year higher education degree, *Bachelor's degree*. All these definitions are exclusive to the United States system.

[2] *Associate in Science* (A.S.) is a first two-year higher education degree granted by a *junior* or *community college*.

[3] A *university* is a higher education institution that offers degrees higher than a Bachelor's degree (including the latter), otherwise called in the United States *graduate studies*.

[4] *Registered Nurse* is a professional qualification granted after 1) a two-year Associate degree or 2) a course of study, with a usual duration of four years, offered by a hospital or 3) a Bachelor's degree in Nursing offered by a college or university, plus a State examination. This concept is different to *licensed practical nurse*, which is a qualification granted after a one- or two-year course of study at hospitals, *community colleges* or adult education programmes.

study with full specialization in nursing. Although the client gave me a previous translation supposedly made by the Spanish Embassy, that document did not include any particular mention, signature or seal to accredit that origin. Yet the client asked me to validate the previous translation. As I showed my surprise at the attempt to validate a two-year *Associate in Science* degree for a three-year *Diplomatura* degree, the client said that her *Associate in Science* had a duration of three years.

After reading the translations presented by the client, I found the following problems:

1) They translated *Degree sought: AS, Major: nursing* as "*Degree sought: Diplomatura, Especialidad en Enfermería*".
2) The professional registration certificate *Registered Nurse*, a professional qualification, was translated as *Diplomada en Enfermería*, an academic degree, fully altering the nature of the document. Further, the license number was omitted in the translated document.
3) The US *Associate in Science* degree is supposed to take two years to be completed but not three. If the client spent one year at the first institution plus two years at the second institution in order to obtain the degree, what she really did was spend one year longer than expected. The US higher education system follows a credit system, not an academic year system (as reformed curricula in Spanish universities currently do). The client converted her workload at the first institution into 34 credits of those required at her second institution; but she did not take the second and third year of the same degree as the one stated at the first institution. As a matter of fact, they were different degrees: *Associate in Science with a major in Nursing* at the first institution and *Associate in Science in Technical Nursing* at her second institution.

The translation assignment was suspicious in more than one way:

- The Spanish translation had no signature, even though the client declared it to have been issued by an embassy
- This translation included numerous irregularities in format (all the individual original documents were included in a single translated document; a shift in the allocation of one of the apostilles, etc.)
- The translation had serious errors and mistakes, omitted information present in the original, etc.
- The client exaggerated the normal duration of the courses in order to justify her application for validation
- The nature of a document had been altered in the translation so as to support the client's aspirations.

My first reason for suspicion was nevertheless the underlying purpose of the translation, that is, to translate US marks into Spanish marks, US degrees into Spanish degrees. My response to the client was to reject the job.

An associated conflict would be as follows. Official translators are empowered to validate other translators' translations, but we do not like to do so and quite often refuse to do so. Clients dislike this, as they think the reason for our refusal is that we distrust their ability to translate (where, as is often the case, they are the ones who have done the translation). However, it takes the official translator as much or even more effort to review another person's translation than to do the translation themselves. Clients in general do not know the norms of official translation and, besides, the client who tries to deceive finds a privileged instrument in a self-made translation.

By definition, the interested party prefers a translation that favours its aspirations and, when it pays, it thinks it is entitled to translation solutions of its choice. That is the case with the translation of academic documents, where the client aspires to the most favourable validation of marks and degrees. Another client proposed an existing translation where a US *Bachelor of Science* (usually of three years duration) was rendered as a *Licenciatura en Ingeniería* (a five-year degree in engineering). Another client may require a mark corresponding to 70% to be translated as a Spanish *notable* (70-89%), even when the pass grade for their system is 70% and for the Spanish system it is 50%. This might also happen in relation to the description of the documents to be translated (a client required a document to be referred to as an *invoice* in the translation when it was really a *bill of exchange*) and so on. On other occasions, clients' requests arouse suspicions of forgery: wrong names or dates, alterations to the original, etc. Proposals for the incomplete translation of a document are not less suspicious. In these situations, the translator can reject the translation assignment, inform the client what their translation would be, or deliver a faithful translation, without further commentary. All these stances jeopardize both payment for the job and the act of translation. The official translator's answer to these situations usually follows a clear ethical guideline. But we can still find other situations where hesitation is possible and various contradictory solutions are available. If, on translating into Spanish a US academic transcript, we do not know the pass grade, are we allowed to reproduce percentages when this pass grade may vary from 60% to 70%?

These situations clearly turn on a contradiction between fidelity and truth. Fidelity to the original document, when combined with cultural differences that act in an implicit way in the interpretation of the text, can lead to inaccurate interpretation of the facts communicated in the original text. That is why the translator of official documents, like any other translator, feels a very powerful urge to act as a bridge, as a communicator between different cultures, offering cultural interpretations as an aid to precise understanding. This stance collides

with the culture of translation rooted in the public administration, which favours opacity or confusion rather than 'infidelity' (text-oriented translation versus
meaning-oriented translation, as we will point out further on).

3.3   The translator's ideology

Official translators must meet the requirements of the original text, of the client, of the recipient, of plausibility, of good style and of fidelity to the original
text, etc. Some of us also add that the translator must submit all their work to a
requirement of truth, which, depending on the case, may lead them to solutions
of equivalence, adaptation or exegesis and, occasionally, to lose a client. Not
all translation scholars would agree here. In Translation Studies it is currently
fashionable to adopt views inherited from literary criticism which hold that objective truth does not exist, that all of us qualify truth according to the filter of
our own ideology (cf. discussions in von Flotow 1991, Arrojo 1994, Venuti
1995, and the overviews in von Flotow 1997, Robinson 1997 and Davis 2001).
These stances propose the visibility of the translator, sometimes involving the
translator conveying their own ideology in the translation. Such practice would
transform reality in a revolutionary direction. On this view, official translators
should, through the alteration or manipulation of the original, contribute to the
liberation of the oppressed.

   In my opinion, this philosophy is not dangerous in official translation; it is
simply unfeasible. The official translator cannot be a public authenticator and
at the same time deny the possibility of objective truth in the translation of documents. The borderline between what official translators may and may not do,
between truth and falseness, is drawn from the liabilities to which they are subject if they stray from truth: civil and criminal liability. Legal mechanisms exist
to decide whether the translator has respected truth.

   Feelings and drives opposed to colonial, sexual exploitation, etc. are certainly present in our field, but they are by no means the only ones to be found at
the heart of the translator. The official translator can face 'exotic' legal situations that give rise to negative reactions (anger or laughter). The professionalism
of the translator represses all these personal impulses; their trade is to make
differences understood instead of suppressing whatever differences may be un-
comfortable. This need to make cultural differences understood may lead the
translator to add explanations without a correlate in the original; these explanations in official translations usually refer to institutional facts and not to cultural
values. It is self-evident that the inclination to translate in favour of the oppressed is just as pernicious as the contrary (also existing): those translators
who take sides for the judge over the accused, for the police over the immigrant, for the powerful over the weak. Their sin is just the same as that of scarlet
pimpernels.

3.4 Across cultural distance

We have observed an increasing flow of documents written in English originating from South Africa, Kuwait, Lebanon, Saudi Arabia, Somalia, Iran, Iraq, Nigeria, Palestine, Gambia, Zambia and Zimbabwe, and also from Hong Kong, Japan, the Philippines, Bangladesh, India, Pakistan, Myanmar and many other countries. The official translator from/into English is usually ready to serve as a bridge between two cultures: one of them English-speaking (normally the United Kingdom and the United States), and the other a second Western culture, such as Spain. The translator might be less prepared for cases like Canada, Australia, New Zealand or South Africa. And they are not usually ready to work between three cultures, as in cases where a country like Pakistan brings a blend of Muslim and Ottoman cultures, which further complicates the English-Spanish interface. Official translators for French also come into contact with Islamic and Arab cultures through the translation of official documents issued in former French colonies.

THE CASE OF PAKISTAN

Translation for Pakistani immigrants and refugees in Spain may be representative of the problems posed by contact with 'exotic' cultures. But it would be inaccurate and unfair to generalize the circumstances of Pakistanis in Spain to that of Pakistanis in Pakistan, the United Kingdom or in general.

Family law in Pakistan is based on the Islamic *sharia* and the administrative system of this country is unfamiliar to most of us. The translation solutions available to overcome these barriers often collide with the special conditions of official translation and with the demands and expectations of the final recipients. In this case the kind of literal translation that authorities favour in their demand for accuracy produces very opaque, not easily understandable versions. And the English official translator in Spain rarely has enough knowledge about something as different and remote as the Urdu language. Their sources of information are not sufficient or reliable enough to allow the translator a full understanding of the document.

The context of translation

Spain has accepted an increasing inflow of Pakistani immigrants in recent years. In some places, Pakistani immigrants have consolidated a well-defined community. Pakistani immigrants require the services of official translators when applying for residence permits, political asylum or Spanish citizenship (quite often through marriage to a female European Union national – almost all such immigrants are men – although cases of family reunification are increasingly common). These immigrants generally arrive in Spain legally and their process of integration seems fairly well organized. However, they have occasionally presented manipulated or forged documents.

The translator's clients in this case are mostly people with a very low educational level (apparently only one fourth of the Pakistani population can read), and they know no Spanish at all (they usually visit the translators accompanied by a fellow Pakistani who serves as an interpreter). Generally speaking, their English is not enough for them to make themselves understood in Spain. Their financial means are extremely limited. The Spanish official translator must be particularly cautious as to the authenticity of the documents presented. The most common documents translated are certificates of birth and death and documents related to family affairs (marriage contracts, repudiation deeds, certificates of family composition, authorizations to marry abroad, and certificates of unmarried status). There are also police and criminal records and, in refugee cases, police statements and letters from lawyers, as well as some academic transcripts, driver licences, and so on. These documents are written in English (which is an official language in Pakistan) although they frequently include some elements of Urdu, which is co-official with English in Pakistan. Pakistani immigrants and refugees also need interpreters for their marriage ceremonies.

Official translation in such circumstances presents various kinds of problems:

Coexistence of two languages: Urdu and English

As far as I know, there is no official translator for the Urdu language in Spain, and we, the Spanish sworn translators, are authorized to translate only those languages for which we have been appointed by the Ministry of Foreign Affairs. A strict application of the rules would thus leave the Urdu words untranslated, and the understanding of the text would be affected negatively. However, a wider interpretation of the rules allows us to consider the presence of the Urdu words in an English text as one of the defining elements of Pakistani English, and official translators of English should thus be authorized to translate the whole text into Spanish. Happily, the authorities have never objected to this latter reasoning.

Once the translator assumes that they must translate Urdu words, new problems arise, the first one being that they do not know Urdu. When the official translator, with the best of intentions, decides to buy an Urdu dictionary, they discover that the entries are written in the Persian script and that searching for information is an all but impossible task for them. The official translator therefore decides to use the client as their informant, which just makes things more complicated. From an ethical and practical point of view, the translator's client is a bad informant. The client has an interest in the process – they are the interested party – and their information might thus be biased or not as objective as desirable. Further, our Pakistani clients usually have difficulty making themselves understood both in English and in Spanish, and they lack any knowledge of Spanish institutions – or indeed of Pakistani institutions. In fact, many of our own questions about Pakistani institutions have received almost as many different answers as people we have consulted, and on many occasions we have addressed very educated people, even diplomatic staff. I must confess that, even for the limited field of the institutions referred to in the documents I have translated, many conceptual areas are still dark regions for me. If, finally, we do manage to translate Urdu words, we discover that there is no consensus about the Spanish versions, neither among translators nor between translators and the recipients of the translations (judges, police). This seriously compromises the efficiency of our work.

Another problem for the Spanish official translator is the type of English used in these documents, which is sometimes impossible to understand even for English speakers from other parts of the world. We find many deviations from the standards we are familiar with, and it is almost impossible to establish whether they correspond to peculiarities of Pakistani English (about which we have no information anyway) or to the linguistic limitations of the officer who drafted the document. Usually, both circumstances coexist, together with a considerable number of typing errors (we may find up to three different spellings for the same word within the same document). An extreme case of 'complicated' English would be the following, found in a paternal authorization to marry abroad:

> To whom ever it me concern mr M.R., I mrs B.B. autorize my son A.R.B. to giet Marrico wihowt objection in spain ano Hearby certify Hak he has not hasrio here en Pakistan o any part of he corlo plus he ir bachiler sin bornwishing wig Blessin toget married soon. Yoisrs Tswly.

Which, I think, meant:

> To whomsoever it may concern, Mr. M.R., I, Mrs. B.B., authorize my son A.R.B. to marry without objection in Spain and hereby certify that he has not been married here in Pakistan or any part of the world and he is a bachelor since birth, wishing with blessings to get married soon. Yours truly.

The writers of this document, apparently, do not easily decipher Roman characters. Normally, codes of ethics would bar the translator from translating this document. But, throughout my professional practice I have accepted to translate whenever I have been certain about what the document means. Here we might refer to the categories of *high-risk information* and *low-risk information* (see, for example, Pym 1996), depending on the risk of inaccuracies resulting in damage for the involved parties, for third parties or for the final recipient.

Defining a piece of information as low-risk allows us to be more daring in our interpretation of it. For example, in a series of birth certificates I repeatedly translated "Informant: Chawkidar" until the reiteration of this very name, *Chawkidar*, made me suspect that there was something fishy going on. Then I discovered that the Urdu word means janitor, and janitors at maternity hospitals are likely to act as informants for birth certificates. A more telling case was a Pakistani document with the word *tarcher*, which stood for *torture*.

Personal names

The normal procedures to indicate which part of a foreign name corresponds to the first name, to the father's last name (first surname in Spain) and to the mother's surname (second surname in Spain) are not applicable to Pakistani personal names, which follow their own tradition. On the one hand, the recipients of the translated document are categorical in their demand for a clear differentiation of the components of the name, in order to achieve precise identification. Pakistani names are included in the original official documents under one sole heading (*name*), and can be composed of two, three or four different elements, whose order does not give us any hint about the nature of the different parts. Parents and their children may not share any element of their names, which may equally happen among brothers and sisters. As for married women, a good number of them take the name *Bibi* or *Begum*, which gives a rather low possibility of identification. When we find several elements in the Pakistani document under the heading 'name' and neither the Spanish official translators nor the Spanish authorities can find a system to assign those parts to first name, first surname and second surname, you can only consult the embassy or even the Pakistani applicant. I have concluded from my own investigation that Spanish judges and police usually consult the Pakistani applicant, which opens interesting possibilities for multiple personalities. This becomes even worse when you consider that the same Urdu name can be transliterated in several different ways within the same document, or in several documents relating to the same person. All things considered, the official translator of English usually chooses to cover their back, giving a literal transcription of the names such as they appear in the original document and renouncing their role as interpreter and bridge between different cultures.

Filiation

According to Islamic law the father is the one to decide filiation, religious confession and kinship. The mother's last name is irrelevant from this point of view. So in Pakistani birth certificates, you find the name of the grandfather, of the midwife, of the informant, but you cannot usually find any heading for the mother's particulars (Moroccan certificates do have the heading, but they still lack the mother's last name). The Western host countries require the full name of the mother. Thus, when Pakistani applicants are involved, Spanish authorities resort to other documents created for a different purpose but which usually do contain the mother's name, i.e. the parental affidavit allowing their sons to marry abroad. At the same time, however, the pressure of growing emigration is making the Pakistani authorities themselves increasingly include mother's name, either under the father's heading or even under a special heading.

Formulas

Documents under Islamic law traditionally use set formulas of salutation referring to God. Very often these are fragments, more or less literal, from the Koran. They are intertextual references, fully meaningful in the Arabic text, but this intertextuality is lost in non-Islamic cultures. For instance:

> In the name of God Almighty. Praise and adoration be to the God, the Great Creator, who founded the basis of existence by association and re-established the human survival by marriage bond, and deep greeting to honourable prophet who confirmed and encouraged this bless tradition.

These ritual formulas do not have any relevance for the legal validity of the document; consequently, the possibility of omitting their translation remains open. Translators from Arabic into Spanish traditionally render all the religious elements in the document with a single sentence: *¡Loor a Dios único!* (*Praise to the only God!*) (*Louanges à Dieu seul*, for French) (Manuel Feria, personal communication).

Administrative and territorial organization

Translating the names of administrative bodies between two different cultures is always difficult. But it can worsen in the case of an official translation, as the pressure exerted on the translator to render literal versions may easily lead to opaque and deceiving results.

In the case of Pakistan, we find the following administrative levels:

	Country
Suba	Province
	Division
Zilah	District
Tehsil	Municipal Committee/Town Committee
Gawn/Quasah/Dahl	Village/Town
Mohallah	Sector/Ward

And the following denominations, which are or may be included in postal addresses:

Gali	Street
Gahr	House
Bazaar	Market
Thaba	Police Station
Chak	P.O. /Post Office

Both Urdu and English words are used to refer to the administrative divisions in Pakistan. We thus find a conceptual system that does not coincide with the Spanish one, and for which we will be short of equivalents in other Western languages. Furthermore, in some contexts the translation of these words will require solutions oriented toward understanding while other contexts will require 'postal address-like' solutions, that is, the transcription of the original words. Quite often administrative elements are often only meaningful when compared *within* a particular culture, but not when compared to administrative elements belonging to another culture. They overlap in substance; they are not coterminous. They can be compared, since the substance is of the same quality, but they cannot be considered exact matches. From this point of view, translation equivalence for these cases may be only approximate even when the original hierarchy can be respected.

Judicial institutions

For a Spanish translator, the figure of the Pakistani 'magistrate' is quite peculiar. He is simultaneously responsible for the police, the representative of government at a *tehsil*, and responsible for the administration of justice (as a 'magistrate' would be at the first-instance court of the English system). This confusion between the executive and the judicial branches of government becomes the main problem for the translator since, in fact, we find in Pakistan two parallel systems of first-instance courts. In Pakistan you can appeal from the 'police' system to the judicial one, but not the other way round.

Much the same problem appears with respect to notaries. In Morocco, for instance, there is a system where with Islamic-law notaries (*aduls*) have jurisdiction for matters governed by the *sharia*, and 'modern notaries' have jurisdiction over all other matters. In other Arab countries, however, *aduls* do not exist and 'modern notaries' follow either the Roman-Germanic system (*muwattiq*, as in Morocco) or the English system of the notary public, depending on the cultural tradition concerned. In countries such as Egypt and Lebanon, there are certain officers at the Ministry of Justice (*maduun* or *mamuur*) who assume part of the functions reserved for *aduls* in family matters.

In Morocco, notarial formalities or acknowledgements must be validated by the judge in charge of notarial affairs at the First Instance Court in order to be valid as public acts; Morocco is a signatory of the Hague Convention. In Pakistan, however, the signature on a document is validated by a notary public; the notary's signature must be validated by a magistrate; the magistrate's by an officer of the Ministry of Foreign Affairs of Pakistan, and the latter's by the Pakistan Embassy in the host country.

The translator and the 'exotic'

Western official translators frequently face *sharia* concepts that are unfamiliar to them. Sometimes, the translator's ideals deeply disagree with concepts like repudiation, *idda* (the waiting period before marrying again), the filiation system, or marriage dowries. That notwithstanding, the translator must show the utmost respect for institutions that regulate the life of hundreds of millions of people, institutions that are intimately linked to the deepest beliefs of those people (their religious faith). Official translators should bear in mind that these institutions are not actually all that far away in time and space from their own (the current applicable French Civil Law also includes the institution of *idda*; legal discrimination against women was in force until about twenty years ago in Spain). Further, Western translators should bear in mind that their client is placing trust in them – in a similar way as the client does with their lawyer – trust that the official translator must not betray. The official translator must not judge clients on the basis of their beliefs or the legal system in which they happen to live. The official translator's attitude must be extremely respectful, polite and neutral.

The professional relationship between the translator and their client

Our Pakistani clients (and others) often do not have the financial means necessary to pay for translation and interpreting services at market prices. Some official translators thus violate standing codes of ethics by working for such clients for well under standard fees, creating unfair competition. Official translation for this group of clients is currently more a case of altruistic aid than professional engagement. Not surprisingly, the translation that the Pakistani receives quite often does not reach the standards of quality and efficiency normal in the trade for the main (and 'wealthier') languages. Steps should be taken in order to guarantee Pakistanis in Spain easy access to the official translation of their documents (perhaps through a rotation system similar of 'translation aid', similar to the 'legal aid' provided in the judicial system). Steps should also be taken to improve the access of these translators to Pakistani culture and its languages, Urdu and English, and to standardize the translation procedures used.

All this will only be possible if dialogue is initiated among Pakistanis, their diplomatic representatives, the judicial and police authorities, and translators.

TRANSLATION CASE

Here we will look at the errors and mistakes incurred in the official translation from Arabic into Spanish of a repudiation deed in Morocco. It runs:

ACTA DE DIVORCIO

Alabado sea Dios,
"A las 15h, del sábado 02 de yumada, De 1405 correspondiente al 23/02/1095, los notarios de derecho musulmán Abdellah Z. y Tahami F., con ejericicio en el Tribunal de 1era Instancia, sección notarial de Tánger, han recibido el testimonio estando depositado en el Registro de conservación nº 2, folio 160, Nº 326, cuyo tenor viene a continuación:
ha comparecido ante los infraescritos Notarios
Mohammed R., hijo de L.L., con domicilio en la Calle M, nº , nacido en 1947, según resulta de su DIN nº – del 19/04/1978,
Quien ha declarado divorciar de su esposa Dña. Karima L., hija de Haj A., mencionada en su acta de nuevas nupcias hecha el 21 de chaoual de 1404 correspondiente al 20/07/1984, nacida en 1984, siendo un tercer, y irrevocable divorcio después de consumir el matrimonio.
La susodicha divorciada ha declarado que no está embarazada, y que ha recibido de su divorciado susodicho 1200 Dh a título de Idda (periodo de retiro legal), y de Muta (continencia), así como otros muebles de la casa, y han convenido que el divorciado debe pagar 250 Dh cada mes como pensión alimenticia de su hija Hind de 8 años de edad.
Las partes conocen el alcance del acto que realizan, de lo cual dan fe los adules que suscriben, así como de que éstas se encuentra en perfecto estado de capacidad legal requerido, y que le son de identidad conocida.
Acta hecha el lunes 11 de Yumada II de 1405 correspondiente al 04 de marzo de 1985.
A continuación figuran las firmas y signos de los dos notarios, así como la diligencia de homologación del Juez encargado de la Notaría, D. Abderrahim G. seguida de su firma, signo y sello de la Sección notarial de Tánger el 18 de yumada de 1405 correspondiente al 11 de marzo de 1985."

In English, this would be:

DIVORCE DEED

Praise to God,
"At 3 p.m., on Saturday, 2nd of Yumada, 1405 corresponding to 23/02/1985, the

Muslim Law notaries, Abdellah Z. y Tahami F., who practise at the First Instance Court, notarial section in Tangier, hereby acknowledge the deposition, registered at the Register of conservation no. 2, page 160, no. 326, whose tenor is the following:

Before the abovementioned Notaries, there has appeared

Mohammed R., son of L.L., resident of Street M., born in 1947, as stated in his National Identity Card no. – issued on 19/04/1978,

Who has declared to have divorced his wife Mrs. Karima L., daughter of Haj A., mentioned at his deed of new marriage executed on 21st of Chaoual, 1404, corresponding to 20/07/1984, born in 1958, this one being their third and irrevocable divorce after having consummated their marriage.

The abovementioned divorced woman has confirmed not to be pregnant and having received from her abovementioned divorcee 1200 Dh by way of Idda (legal retirement period), and Muta (continence), as well as other pieces of furniture from their home, and they have agreed that the divorced man must pay 250 Dh per month as maintenance of their daughter Hind, 8 years old.

Both parties are conscious of the effect of the act they perform. The aduls acknowledge their full established legal capacity to do so, and declare they know them. In witness whereof the aduls set their hand and seal to this deed, made on Monday on 11th of Yumada II, 1405 corresponding to 4th of March, 1985.

The signatures and marks of both notaries follow, as well as the validation of the judge in charge of the Notary's Office, Abderrahim G., which is followed by his signature, sign and mark of the Notarial Section Notarial in Tangier on 18th of Yumada II, 1405 corresponding to 11th of March 1985."

The problems that we find in this translation relating to the cultural differences are as follows (cf. El Alami and Hinchcliffe1996):

divorce	The subject matter is not a divorce but a repudiation (*talaq*), even though in English documents it is common to find the term 'divorce' (*tatliq* or judicial divorce; *jul* or divorce in consideration of payment by the wife).
Praise to God	This is a set formula empty of a meaning in itself; many translators omit it.
Yumada II, *chaoual*	Dates of the *hijrah* (Muslim era); unnecessary; many translators omit it.
Islamic Law notaries	In this case, they are the same people as *aduls* and notaries.
Idda	The following translations are possible: *Idda* (Morocco), *Iddat* (Pakistan), period/time of widowhood (if influenced by the French Civil Code), waiting period of 90 days (inaccurate; it really corresponds to three menstrual cycles), period of legal continence, plus explicative and multiple translation solutions.
Muta	Conceptual mistake; it is not a period of continence (not even *Idda* is strictly this) but of economic compensation to the wife as a consequence of repudiation.
deed of new marriage	Misleading solution; it refers to a new marriage to the same wife after a repudiation; "deed of restoring marriage" would be preferable .
Judge in charge of the Notary's Office	Unlikely and inaccurate; it is the Judge of the Court of First Instance in charge of Notarial Affairs.

To avoid these traps, some basic knowledge of *sharia* is necessary, even though the complexity of Islamic law is increased by the coexistence of various schools and interpretations. An introduction to Islamic law especially for translators without Arabic, Urdu, etc. would be most welcome. I think that the curriculum for English, French and German translators and interpreters should include some contents related to this topic. If we are not familiar with the terms and concepts and no assistance is available, we should not really accept such jobs. Effort should also be made to ensure that the main translation solutions are standardized among translators, clients and the administration. This standardization should include the revision of all the traditional fossilized solutions (see 7.1 below) for the sake of better, more accurate translations.

Another view of exoticism

Legal texts in the Maghreb related to non-Islamic law are usually inspired by French texts or are even translations from French. Something similar happens with eastern Arab countries, whose legislation is clearly based on English Common Law. A strong Western heritage can also be found in administrative divisions in the Arab world. When translating some legal or administrative texts from Arabic into a Western language, we may really be translating from 'exotic' Western legal systems, which the translator may or may not know sufficiently well. The same may be true when working with other languages, such as Turkish or Farsi.

Suggested activities

1) Provide an official translation for the academic transcript included in the Appendix according to a 'validation strategy'.
2) Provide an official translation for the same transcript without seeking equivalents for grades and degrees.
3) Tell someone who knows English to translate their academic transcript into English. Compare it to your own translation. Edit your friend's translation to turn it into an acceptable official translation that you can validate.
4) Each member of the class gives an informative and complete translation of the joint-venture contract included in the Appendix. These translations are revised by the class, discussing which of the parties to the contract is favoured or harmed by each error or mistake, if any.
5) Make a basic bilingual glossary of Muslim marriage and divorce concepts. The column corresponding to the non-Arabic language should consist of solutions fit for official translation.
6) Translate the Philippine gold certificate, included in the Appendix, into standard English.
7) Which elements in the Letter of Credit included in Chapter 5 suggest that English is not the author's first language?
8) Which elements in this Letter of Credit suggest that the author's first language is not written with the Roman alphabet?

4. Documents

4.1 Types

Any type of text can be the object of official translation, since any activity or information may be the subject matter or one of the elements of a claim, a suit, a report, a contract, or any other legal act. Let us see some examples taken from professional practice, errors included.

Example 1. A suicide note

Mum:
I love you very much but I can't go further. I don't have enoughf strength. Be a good girl. I hope Daddy drop deth one of this and goes to hell with his disgusting girlfriends.

Example 2. A private letter

This is very difficult because if my wife finds out I'm finish. She'll take everything from me. I would not have had sex with you if you were going to get pregnant. You told me there was no way you could get pregnant.

Example 3. A scientific paper

Interesting information is provided by Table 10 taken from a Canadian study which covers an observation period of 29 years and analyses 428 deaths of spinal cord injured patients according to causes of death. Renal insufficiency and heart/circulatory diseases were the main causes of death (5.2%).

Example 4. An academic transcript

Course title	Crse nr	Hrs	grade	Pnts
Fall sem 1992	Boulder Campus			
Graduate School	Spanish			
Port for Span Speaker	Port 2350-801	3.0	A	12.0 G
Crit Approach Hispani Lit	Span 71300-001	3.0	B+	9.9 G
Sem-20C Span Amer Liter	Span 7320-001	3.0	B+	9.9 G
Arr 9.0 Earned 9.0 Gpahts 31.80	GPA 3.533			
Cumulative credits:				

Tr Hrs	Cu Hrs	Tot hrs	Qual hrs	Qual Pts	GPA
Grad Sem	0.0	9.0	9.0 9.0	31.80	3.533

Example 5. Academic documentation

Contents
Preface
    1. Photography, Films and Filters
    2. Orientation and Study of Aerial Photographs
    3. Photo Scale and Stereoscopic Parallax
    4. Stereograms, Shadow Heights, and Areas
    5. Flight Planning
    6. Planimetric and Topographic Mapping

Example 7. An administrative document

Furthermore, a claimant may be disqualified if he has:-
lost his employment through his misconduct (the term is used in its industrial
sense and includes breaches of discipline of work rules, or conduct inconsistent
with the fulfilment of conditions of service or which renders him incapable of
performing his work efficiently);

Example 8. A traffic accident report

Sitting in middle lane waiting to move across to left lane slow moving traffic
(very heavy) when a red car moved across to centre lane and hit my N.F. wheel.
No damage Artic. Very small dent on her right wing.

Example 9. Company statutes

The Executive Committee shall have executive control of the institution in the
name and in behalf of the Board of Trustees and shall act for the Board during
the interim that the Board is no in session. It shall make a full report of its acts
and proceedings to the Board at the regular meetings of that body.

Example 10. A judicial sentence

The defendant is sentenced as provided in pages 2 through 5 of this judgement.
The sentence is imposed pursuant to the Sentencing Reform Act of 1984.
The defendant has been found not guilty on accounts 1,2,3&8 of the supersed-
ing indictment and is discharged as to such counts.

Example 11. A financial statement

Consolidated statement of financial position

Assets
Current Assets
Accounts Receivable
Materials and Supplies
Deferred Income Taxes
Other Current Assets
Total Current Assets

Example 12. Deed of trust

Settle any capital on all or any one or more of the Beneficiaries and any settlement made by the Trustees under this present power upon or for the benefit of
any or more of the Beneficiaries as aforesaid may be created in and under the
law on any part of the world (being a part of the world the local law whereof
recognises settlements of the kind proposed to be made)...

Example 13. A will

I GIVE DEVISE AND BEQUEATH all my said real and personal estate unto
my Trustees hereinafter named UPON TRUST to sell call in and convert into
money the same or such part thereof as shall not consist of money and to hold
the proceeds of such sale calling in and conversion and my ready money (after
paying thereout my funeral and testamentary expenses and debts) in trust for
such of them my daughters ... and ... as shall be living at my death and if all
survive me then in equal parts absolutely...

This list is illustrative only of diversity; it does not try to cover all the documents that may be subject to official translation. However, some types of
documents are more likely than others, depending very much on the area in
which we live. Here are the most common types:

- births, marriages and deaths
- divorce
- academic
- agreements and guarantees
- powers of attorney
- wills
- adoption
- companies
- rogatory letters
- sentences and resolutions
- identification.

4.2 Information and functions

Original communication act vs. translation act

Traditionally, translating is viewed as the transmission of a message from one language to another. This concept is too simplistic for the analysis of the official translation process. The main differences between the source communication act and the translation act are:

- the recipients are different in each case
- in other kinds of translation, there is no blank form to be completed.

This second point is important because source-culture blank forms are originally intended for the interested parties, informants or civil servants. They are written for the purposes of communication between an expert and a layman, since the final documents are always directed to specialists in the public administration. In the case of the US, and increasingly in the UK, the difference is even more evident since there is a tendency to use plain English in administrative documents. In an American birth certificate, for example, we will find 'Usual residence of mother (Where does mother live?)'. In other words, the documents are written in such a way as to make them generally easier to understand. This helps to guarantee the applicant's rights and prevents problems arising due to a lack of understanding.

We propose to call this kind of source a *virtual document*. This would be a non-existent document derived from the union of a blank form and the particulars of an event, or the document as it would have been written originally had the particulars been known. The style of this ideal virtual document is easy to understand. Gone are all the elements in the form that are not linked to actual data, such as headings and unanswered alternatives, along with instrumental elements such as instructions and warnings. A translation could conceivably be based on the resulting virtual document (the 'essential information') rather than the real one.

At the same time, the translated document should itself be intended for the public administration. It should thus be more uniform in style, lose its colloquial elements, and find the solutions that are ideal for the final recipient. The final recipient of the source document was a foreign administration, and each administration has its own set of requirements, norms and customs that they expect documents to meet. However, if the source text does not include information that the foreign administration considers essential, such as the particulars of the mother in a Pakistani birth certificate, there will be a problem. The contrary may occur if the document offers information that a foreign administration does not consider relevant, such as race and caste, in the Pakistani example. In all of these cases, the important point is whether the document will be accepted, rather than the exact equivalence of the translation. Acceptability is established by the receiving administration. Pakistani birth certificates, for example, usually require a certification of unmarried status in order to be accepted in Spain, which means an authorization to be married signed by the mother.

The 'virtual document' would thus ideally include all the elements that will enable it to be accepted by the receptor authorities in the target culture.

Functions of the information

In our texts we have found the following functions and information, as well as the elements that transmit them:

❑ The document's performative function, in which the utterance performs the document's purpose: 'I certify that', in a certificate, is the main act in Ferrara's (1980a, 1980b) sequence of subordinate speech acts.

❑ referential functions (informative)
  ➢ information that identifies the document
    • publication of the form (institution or business that has printed it)
    • name of the document
    • reference code (the document's identification number or alphanumeric code)
    • the relevant regulation (for example, what Births and Deaths Registration Ordinance it follows)
    • the institution that issues the document (sender)
    • the name of the person who issues or certifies (sender)
    • the status of the person who issues or certifies
    • place and date of issue
  ➢ information identifying the documented event
    • registration number
    • registration date/academic period
    • informant or witnesses
  ➢ information defining the documented event
    • type of event
  ➢ information describing the documented event
    • participants
    • place, date, and time
    • result (medical information, academic marks)

❑ Directive functions (part of the appellative or operative function)
    • instructions
    • clarifications (exegesis)
    • warnings

❑ Internal reference function
    • textual cohesion elements (internal remissions, pages, letter-headings, etc.)

TYPES OF INFORMATION

We can illustrate the above functions by applying them to the birth certificate reproduced in the Appendix. This would give us something like the following:

U.K. BIRTH CERTIFICATE
➤ A. IDENTIFYING THE DOCUMENT (REFERENTIAL)
A.1 Document name
Certified Copy of an Entry of Birth B. Cert
A.2 Document reference number
DQ 311776
A.3 Relevant regulations
Pursuant to...
A.4 Issuing Body
Registration District... RBD [Heading]
A.5 Person who issues/certifies
Gladys H. Hider
A.6 Occupation of the person who issues/certifies
Registrar of Births and Deaths
A.7 Place and date of issue
13-6-98
A.8 Edition of form
Printed by authority of the Registrar General
➤ B. IDENTIFYING THE DOCUMENTED EVENT (REFERENTIAL)
B.1 Entry number
248
B.2 Registration date/academic period
12/6/98
B.3 Informant (witnesses, in other documents)
Name, signature, status, address
➤ C.DEFINING THE DOCUMENTED EVENT (REFERENTIAL)
C.1 Type of event
Birth
➤ D. DESCRIBING THE DOCUMENTED EVENT (REFERENTIAL)
D.1 Participants in the event
Child/interested party (name, sex)
Father (name, signature, age, address, occupation) Mother (name, maiden name, age, address)
Informant (witnesses, in other documents): (name, signature, occupation, address)
D.2 Place and date (time) of the event
8/6/68, Alexandra Park Road
D.3 Result of the event: medical report/grades
[Applicable to other documents]
➤ E. PERFORMING THE DOCUMENTATION (REFERENTIAL)
I do hereby certify that this is a true copy of the entry... The notary's legalizations and the Apostille of Her Majesty's Principal Secretary of State for Foreign and Commonwealth Affairs.
➤ F. HELPING TO UNDERSTAND AND COMPLETE THE FORM (INSTRUCTIONS)
F.1 Instructions
Insertion of name in space 17 of Birth Register The Statutory fee...
F.2 Clarifications (exegetics)
[Applicable to other documents]
F.3 Warnings
Caution: ...
➤ G. OTHER: ELEMENTS FOR INTERNAL REFERENCE OR OF TEXT COHESION
*See note overleaf Epigraphs or box numbers

Relevance of information

In the text we have analyzed, some of the information was relevant in the source document for reference purposes, comprehension, or for validation of the original, but is no longer relevant in the translation. This happens, or may happen, with:

a) References that identify the source document, unless they could be used to confirm the truth of the document or to check the authenticity of the facts with the original authorities;
b) References that identify the documented event, for the same reasons as above;
c) Part of the information describing the documented event, including information that originally had a validating function, such as identification of the authority present, the informant or witnesses, and medical information for vital statistics;
d) Performative information or the main speech act;
e) Information given in order for the document to be understood and completed correctly;
f) Cross-references and cohesive elements within the original document.

These elements need not be considered parts of the 'virtual document' that is to be translated. This means that shortened versions of a document can also be considered legitimate translations, as in the case of multilingual documents. An example would be a multilingual birth certificate for the European Union, or the translation of a driver's licence issued by the Spanish Royal Automobile Club (RACE). It would be a matter of discerning which information is needed in order for the legal act to be recognized. The translation could then be of only those elements. The translation of a birth certificate, for example, could include the following information:

Sender
Institution that issued the document
Textual act
Name of child
Sex
Place of birth
Date of birth
Father's name
Mother's name
Reference to birth's entry
Recipient
A validation of the authenticity of the above facts that would be acceptable to the authority being addressed.

All the translations of RACE'S driving licences use the same form, which reads:

RACE
Certified translation of a driver's licence
Issued in:
Licence number:
Place and date of issue:
Valid until:
Permit holder:
Equivalence to Spanish licence:
To whom it may concern:
The above is a faithful transcription of the essential data given in the driver's licence described, which is to be presented at the Traffic Department in
This is an official certification in accordance to article 267, section 111, of the Traffic Code in force.
Photocopy of the licence enclosed.

The following could be an example of translation at a level 'lower' than the source text, taken from an American birth certificate. It reflects what we mean by translation of a virtual document:

ORIGINAL

4 SEX
masculine   feminine
5a THIS BIRTH
single   twin   triplet
5b IF TWIN OR TRIPLET (This child born)
1st   2nd   3rd
6 DATE OF BIRTH
    (Month)   (Day)   (Year)
       7   5   1954

BACKTRANSLATION OF FIRST TRANSLATION

4.   SEX: Masculine [crossed box].- Feminine [blank box]
5a.   THIS BIRTH IS: Single [crossed box].- Twin [blank box].- Triplet [blank box]
5b.   IF TWIN OR TRIPLET, this child was born first [blank box].- Second [blank box].- Third [blank box]
6.   DATE OF BIRTH: Day: 5.- Month: 7.- Year: 1954

BACKTRANSLATION OF SECOND TRANSLATION

4. SEX: masculine
5. KIND OF BIRTH: single
6. DATE OF BIRTH: 5-7-1954

The second translation only reflects the information that remains relevant once the form has been completed. That is, it is of the virtual document.

Whether information is relevant depends on the level of risk involved if it is not translated completely. Not all the information in a given text is equally *sensitive* or *high-risk*. In the translation of a birth certificate, the name of the midwife is not as important as the name of the child, the parents, or the date of birth.

Relevance of the validation

So far we have included validation formalities as part of the information in the source document that might not remain relevant in the translation. Official documents and their translation are subject to a series of validations, authentications or certifications. Each validation at a higher level implies that a validation has been made previously or at a lower level. Therefore, each successive validation makes the previous ones unnecessary. The Hague Apostille on a foreign document signifies that the source document is authentic and can make any mention of previous formalities superfluous. Information about the Registrar who made the first entry or the identity of the doctor who attended and certified the birth may not be relevant in the translation. It is important to note that each culture follows different criteria as to the requirements that a document must meet.

Relevance of the instructions

The instructions for completing the original form correctly are no longer relevant once the form has been completed. These instructions can be very long, as in the case of British birth certificates, in which detailed descriptions of how to correct erroneous data may occupy the entire back page of a document. The same thing may occur in academic transcripts when describing calendars or grading scales. In this case, some of the information may remain relevant in the translation, such as the grading system or the value of the courses in relation to the academic program.

Relevance of internal references

The references internal to the source text will only be necessary if the translation is to be checked against the source text. If the internal references are retained in the translation, however, their numbers and letters must correspond with the source text.

Suggested activities

1) Add, to the list included in this chapter, five new cases of non-legal documents that might be translated officially. Describe situations in which their official translation might be needed.
2) Divide the US death certificate in the Appendix according to the different kinds of information it contains. Provide an official translation for it, keeping just the information relevant for a Civil Registry in your country.
3) Compare the fees for official translations of the British birth certificate in Appendix for 1) a complete translation (face and back of the document) and 2) a partial translation (only the face).
4) Write or find a love letter written by a man talking about a future marriage (search on the Internet). Imagine a pregnancy has resulted from that relationship and a claim for recognition of children born out of wedlock is filed. Provide an official translation of the letter to be used as proof in court, paying special attention to terms of endearment, feelings, formality and promises.

5. The Official Translator as Jurilinguistic Expert

Official translators have privileged linguistic knowledge that extends beyond the rendering of the meanings of the original. They can assess the origin and authenticity of the language used and they can ideally detect intended ambiguity and nuances of expression. Official translators also have privileged *non-linguistic* knowledge on a variety of levels. They are familiar with the legal systems, the peculiarities of different kinds of documents, and the cultural background of the countries involved. Official translators can be required to report on changes of personal names (usually after the foreigner's naturalization); they can also inform on legal aspects of the foreign culture (such as the nature of repudiation in Islamic law), usually at the lawyer's request.

Sometimes legal translators contribute their knowledge voluntarily, out of the loyalty they feel toward their clients, or as a contribution to truth and justice. This is the case when the official translator advises the client on possible legal problems in the document to be translated (for instance, if the document says that the injured party is the liable party). On other occasions, the translator may be required (usually by a judge) to assess a problem in a document (for instance, to establish whether it is a letter of exchange or an invoice). The translator may also be required to give their opinion on the authenticity of a document. Let us see a document that requires the translator's expert opinion prior to translation, in relation to content as much as to its wording and spelling.

TRANSLATION CASE

Specimen only
LETTER OF CREDIT "COMMERCIAL"
To: Banco P.E.
No: ....
From: Lloyds........London
Branch sorting code: ....
Test   On USD 1.180.000.00   Date: Feb-09-2000
Please advise this Letter of Credit to ....("the Beneficiary") through Banco P.E.
No: ......
By order of "..........., Israel (the Applicant), we hereby establish our irrevocable and transferable Letter of Credit no. .... Dated Feb-8-2000 in favour of ...., Spain, for a maximum amount of USD 1.180.000.00 covering credit facilities which the Beneficiary has granted to ...., Spain in relation to the contract no. 1- (one) between ...., Spain, and ....,

Israel, for the acquisition of -5- containers of Narlboro Light.

This Letter of Credit is avalabele for payment at our counters only at maturity on 72 hours of working days in terms and presentation of all the following documents:

1. The Beneficiary's signed statement stating that the credit facilities granted to ...., Spain have become due and remain unpaid after 72 hours after the applicant expert sigen receiving one container at the time
2. Patial shipment are allowed. One container will deliver monthly
3. Signed commercial invoice original and 5 copies certifying that the goods are Phillip Moris made
4. Packing list
5. Certification of origin

Covering: 5-containers of cigarets Marlboro Light USD 136.000 per container. All documents to be forwarded top us in one lot by SWIFT. We irrevocably undertake to accept the abovemntioned documents presented under this letter of credit and to effect payment thereof in accordance with your instructions, provided that all documents presented are in strict conformity with the terms of this credit.

This credit is subject to UC and P for Documentary Credit (1993 Revisson) ICC Publicatin 500.

Confirmation will allow.

[signed by the Importer]

We the beneficiary agree and accept the above letter of credit which is being opened in our favour. We are inform and agree that the text may be modifying by the opening bank without Changing the meaning and the constraction and condition in this letter of credit. We accept the text on the letter of credit and the modifications thereof.

Note the following peculiarities:

- This supposed letter of credit uses some English that is quite strange; the problems the writer has with spelling suggest a native speaker of a language that is not written with the Roman alphabet. In any case, the language does not correspond to what you could expect from an officer of a major English bank.
- The document is marked as 'specimen'; it should not have been executed.
- The test (reference number) that identifies the transaction is compulsory but it is blank in this document.
- The letter of credit is not signed by the issuing bank but by the principal, the importer.

- You can find contents related to a sales transaction, to a guarantee and to a credit facility, all of them combined.

The letter of credit turned out to be a fraud, as the translator had advised their client.

Rendering service as an intercultural expert can be conflictive. In some countries, like Spain, a court interpreter cannot work as an interpreter and as an expert in the same case. Especially problematic – with technical and ethical implications – is the case of interpreters at police stations and courts who are required to ascertain the country of origin of immigrants from their speech or through questions about cultural matters.

Suggested activities

1) Provide an official translation for the suicide note at the beginning of chapter 4. Assess whether the note was really written by a nine-year old child or whether it could be a forgery made by an adult.
2) Guess the nationality of the author of the above-mentioned Letter of Credit.
3) Read the non-circumvention and non-disclosure agreement included in the Appendix. Identify anything non-idiomatic or incorrect and revise it. Have you found any influence from a language other than English?
4) Find a Trust Deed for participation in an investment society. Advise your client (the would-be Trustor) on the advisability and consequences of signing it.

6. Different Ways of Translating

6.1 Adequacy conditions

Austin (1962) established a series of 'fortune' or success conditions for performative utterances that must be met or the speech act will fail. Ferrara (1980a and 1980b) has extended the concept of speech acts to sequences of speech acts, developing fortune conditions into wider 'appropriateness' conditions. He considers that speech acts are inserted into sequences and then into the specific communicative activities that are taking place. Something similar would seem to be at stake when Nord (1997:35) describes the 'adequacy' of a translation in the following terms:

> This means the translator cannot offer the same amount and kind of information as the source-text producer. What the translator does is offer another kind of information in another form [...]. Within the framework of *Skopostheorie*, 'adequacy' refers to the qualities of a target text with regard to the translation brief: the translation should be 'adequate' to the requirements of the brief.

We think the above contributions can be combined to propose certain adequacy conditions for official translation. These would establish on the one hand, the conditions that must be met by the translation act so that it can take place and not fail, and on the other hand, the conditions required for the communicative act to be effective.

Success conditions

Success conditions are thus those that, if not met, will annul the viability of the translation act. The first two conditions that we propose are professional considerations, while the third is a question of ethics:

1. An official translation must be acceptable to the final recipient (the administrative authority). The following elements can be decisive in deciding a refusal:
    *   the information transmitted is not relevant
    *   the information is incomprehensible
    *   the information is incomplete
    *   the translation has been performed in an irregular way
    *   the applicable legal norms have been broken
    *   incorrect tenses and form have been used
    *   the functions of the text have not been respected

- there are difficulties with identification
- the translation is ambiguous
- the original text is not valid
- the translated text is not plausible as a document to be given to the authority
- the style is inappropriate.

2. The official translation has to be acceptable to the client (when the client is not the administrative authority).
3. The official translation must be true to the facts it is transmitting.

Effectiveness conditions

Effectiveness conditions are then those that will affect the suitability or the quality of the translation if they are not met:

1. The translator's exegesis must be clearly differentiated from the information given in the source document (within square brackets).
2. In addition to the text, other informative elements present in the source text must be included, such as illustrations or signatures (within square brackets).
3. All the elements of the source text must be indicated, such as any changes that may have been made, information that has been erased or added, damage, illegible words, or incomplete text (within square brackets).
4. Any elements of the source text that may be due to an attempt to falsify the original document must also be noted (within square brackets).
5. The official translation must offer the client the most cost-effective solutions. This means that the translated text should be as brief as requirements allow.

Translation by default and other translation alternatives

When listing the adequacy conditions for communication in official translation, we have also established certain success conditions. We will now centre on the success condition that the translation must be acceptable to the final recipient, the administrative authority. If an official translation is perfect in every respect but does not meet this condition, it will not become an official translation and therefore it will have failed.

At the microtextual level, *translation by default* means that the translation has been performed in the most predictable way, which is the most usual way (Mayoral and Muñoz 1997).

At the macrotextual level, or the 'way to translate the entire text', we call *translation by default* the most predictable way to perform a translation. It meets the expectations of the recipient and, if not followed by the translator, causes perplexity or is perceived as strange (cf. the notion of 'expectancy norms' in Chesterman 1997). Every translation task has a way to be translated by default if instructions are not given or are incomplete. It corresponds to an 'implicit' translation brief or 'conventional assignment' (Nord 1997:30-1). The translator must know what to do in a situation in which no specifications are given; it should form part of their training. Translation by default can change over time. It can undergo modifications due to the constant minor transgressions committed by translators and initiators, or changes in norms.

In official translation, translation by default must be approached differently than it would be in other kinds of translation.

The Spanish authorities have not yet defined what they would consider acceptable in an official translation. The law regulating professional translation states that certifications must be a 'faithful and full translation'. Those translators who do not wish to run the risk of having their translations rejected try to adapt to the following rules:

- The translation is unabridged, in that no meaning has been added to the original or omitted.
- Neither exegetic nor multiple formulations are applied; only established, literal, solutions are used.
- The focus is on the source culture (Mayoral and Muñoz 1997).
- The source text is the blueprint for the order, format, and structure of the translation.
- Emphasis is placed on what is generally called formal and semantic fidelity to the source text. This is the type of translation that comes under the heading 'literal', 'word for word', 'semantic', or 'documentary'. As Nord (1997:47) says:

> The first [**documentary translation**] aims at producing in the target language a kind of *document* of (certain aspects of) a communicative interaction in which a source-culture sender communicates with a source-culture audience via the source text under source-culture conditions [...]. The target text, in this case, is a text about a text, or about one or more particular aspects of a text.

In official translation, this approach constantly endangers the translator's ability to meet all of the effectiveness conditions (such as relevance, understanding, lowest possible fees, and identification). It can even affect the success condition of the translation's truthfulness.

In fact, in every official translation the translator feels the tension between different ways of translating and different 'fidelities'; they must come to intermediate translation solutions. They must play with the administration's margins of acceptability in the areas that are not regulated by law, but without going beyond them. The occasional decision not to translate an informative element is already part of professional practice, since the translator knows, both instinctively and from experience, what information is superfluous.

Translating by default is changing and will continue to change. It is to be hoped that the public authorities will learn more about translation and that the profession will actively participate in that process. Professional translators must become aware of the instruments they use, of the different approaches to translating, and of the resulting effectiveness of the communication process. This is essential not only for the acceptability of the translation but also to its intrinsic qualities as an instrument of communication.

6.2. Constraints

6.2.1 Legal norms

Legal norms present the highest degree of obligation for the official translator. There are *general legal rules* that are not specific to official translation and apply to any citizen and to different spheres of life. The breach of these rules may imply civil and even criminal liabilities for translators. Some of these norms are confidentiality, helping in the commission of crimes or not informing about them, and falseness and damages derived from inadequate renderings of the original. There are other liabilities such as losing or damaging the original documents, or damages caused by delays.

Usually, translating or interpreting for the courts is considered an aggravating circumstance: the guilt of an expert working for the legal system is thought to be greater than that of 'normal' translators.

There may also be *specific legal norms* that apply exclusively to official translation. In Spain, a law establishes the exact wording of the translator's certification and norms concerning the seal. The breach of these rules can cause the translation to be invalid and unacceptable for the public authorities or other recipients. Liabilities derived from damages may occur.

Both kinds of legal norms – general and specific – must be respected by official translators.

The way to avoid the consequences of legal liability is to take out an insurance policy that covers professional services, specifically translation. Most main insurers offer this kind of security, which only provides partial cover for risks.

Many people think that the responsibility of an official translator is much greater than that of other kinds of translators. Official translators are thought to handle documents of decisive importance for huge sums of money, the freedom of people, the paternity of children, and so on. Further, our proximity to law enforcement officers and the courts perhaps makes us feel particularly vulnerable. But responsibility can also be tremendously high for other kinds of translation: technical manuals, international legislation, and community interpreting may all be high-risk activities.

6.2.2 Ethical norms: professional vs. personal

I think a distinction can be established between the ethical principles of the individual (personal decisions about what is right and wrong) and those that belong to a group, which are collective (as is the case with professional associations and their decisions about what is right and wrong). The latter is what English usually calls 'codes of ethics' and which other languages call either 'codes of ethics' (in different words) or, often, 'deontological codes'. We should not confuse these concepts. Personal ethics affects only the particular individual; personal ethical principles cannot or should not be imposed on a whole community of people, not even on a profession. Professional ethics, on the other hand, belongs to the sphere of professional organizations: the Society of Public Translators of the City of Buenos Aires, the International Federation of Translators, the local associations of translators or associations of official translators. Professional ('deontological') rules or principles are binding for the members of the corresponding association and the consequence of breaching them is expulsion from the related association. Special committees within the association or professional society judge these cases. They usually include the following principles, transcribed from the Translator's Charter (approved by the FIT Congress at Dubrovnik in 1963, and amended in Oslo on 9 July 1994):

Section I
General Obligations of the Translator

1. Translation, being an intellectual activity, the object of which is the transfer of literary, scientific and technical texts from one language into another, imposes on those who practise it specific obligations inherent in its very nature.
2. A translation shall always be made on the sole responsibility of the translator, whatever the character of the relationship of contract that binds him/her to the user.
3. The translator shall refuse to give a text of which he/she does not approve, or which would be contrary to the obligations of his/her profession.
4. Every translation shall be faithful and render exactly the idea and the form of the original – this fidelity constituting both a moral and legal obligation of the translator.
5. A faithful translation, however, should not be confused with a literal translation, the fidelity of a translation not excluding an adaptation to make the form, the atmosphere and deeper meaning of the work felt in another language and country.
6. The translator shall possess a sound knowledge of the language from

which he/she translates and should, in particular, be a master of that into which he/she translates.

7. He/she must likewise have a broad general knowledge and know sufficiently well the subject matter of the translation and refrain from undertaking a translation in a field beyond his/her competence.

8. The translator shall refrain from any unfair competition in carrying out his/her profession; in particular, he/she shall strive for equitable remuneration and not accept any fee below that which may be fixed by law and regulations.

9. In general, he/she shall not seek nor accept work under conditions humiliating to himself/herself or his/her profession.

10. The translator shall respect the legitimate interests of the user by treating as a professional secret any information, which may come into his/her possession as a result of the translation entrusted to him/her.

11. Being a 'secondary' author, the translator is required to accept special obligations with respect to the author of the original work.

12. He/she must obtain, from the author of the original work or from the user, authorization to translate a work, and must furthermore respect all other rights vested in the author.

The definition in point 1 is too general for official translation; points 11 and 12 are not applicable to this kind of translation. Point 9 is very subjective and thus unnecessary and not applicable. For a discussion of point 8, related to fees, see Section 10.1 below; the point does not correspond to professional reality any longer. Point 7 (elsewhere formulated as 'The translator shall not accept any commission which exceeds his/her competence') conflicts with common professional practice as well.

Within the document *Best Practice in Court Interpreting* published by the FIT (Fédération Internationale des Traducteurs) we find the following on translation assignments:

1. Accepting an assignment
The client and the translator shall agree on the timetable of the translation assignment and on the fees, etc. in advance and shall confirm the assignment in writing, whenever necessary. The translator shall not accept an assignment and then request another translator to take it on without consulting with the client.

2. Performing an assignment
2.1 The translator shall apply due diligence when doing the translation, consulting whatever sources necessary (dictionaries, encyclopaedias, experts, etc.).
2.2 The translator shall produce the translation in keeping with legal requirements (length of lines/page, proper certification) and shall settle his/her fees similarly.
2.3 The translator shall consult with the client should there be obvious

ambiguities and/or mistakes in the original text and never make any
corrections himself/herself without previous consultation.
2.4 The translation shall be of high standard and neat in appearance.

If this is a deontological code for official translation, the obvious conclusion is
that there should not be any such thing. It is irrelevant, too obvious, or non-
applicable to current professional practices. Free exercise of translation can more
easily adapt to a changing profession.

The most specific current code in Spain is that of the Catalan Association.
Our own translation of this runs as follows:

CODE OF ETHICS
OF THE SWORN TRANSLATOR AND INTERPRETER
Preamble
The aim of this Code is to state the principles guiding the attitude and the
behaviour of the sworn interpreter and translator in the development of
his/her specific endeavour and endowing the collective with the norms
of professional ethics. These ethical norms do not exclude others which
are not specifically mentioned but which derive from an honourable and
correct professional practice. This Code is not deemed to permit whatever it does not forbid.
Scope
Art.1 – These norms apply to the practice of the profession of sworn
translator and interpreter.
Art. 2 – The general practice of the profession must be conscious and
honourable and fidelity to truth must be for sworn interpreters and translators their permanent norm of behaviour and the goal of their
performance. Technique should not be used in order to distort truth.
Art. 3 – Undertakings, both written and oral, must be considered binding.
Art. 4 – Sworn interpreters and translators should not intervene in businesses from which they do not keep absolute independence.
Art. 5 – Sworn interpreters and translators must not intervene when their
professional performance:
a) allows, protects or facilitates improper or punishable acts;
b) may be used to confound or abuse bona fide third parties;
c) may be used in detriment of public interest or of the interest of the
profession or to deceive the law.
Art. 6 – Sworn interpreters and translators must not interrupt the performance of their professional services without reasonable prior
notification, unless circumstances expressly forbid this notification.
Art. 7 – Sworn interpreters and translators, whichever the field of their
activity might be, must respect and apply the norms and the spirit of this
Code.
Art. 8 – Sworn translators and interpreters must abide by the laws, and
loyally observe them.

Art. 9 – Sworn interpreters and translators must comply with the rulings of the Association, both in their meaning and in their wording.

Art. 10 – Any translation, report or ratification, written or spoken, must be faithful, clearly and precisely expressed. Sworn interpreters and translators must assume full liability for the contents of the translation signed by them, and they cannot justify themselves on the grounds of errors or mistakes attributable to other people under their direction or inaccuracies contained in the original text.

Art. 11 – Sworn interpreters and translators should not sign translations from or to a language for which they are not authorized, nor should they sign those translations which have not been performed by them or under their supervision.

Art. 12 – Sworn interpreters and translators should not allow any other person to practise in their name, nor make non-professionals appear as professionals.

Art. 13 – Sworn interpreters and translators should not collaborate with learning institutions which use deceitful publicity or improper procedures to perform their activities or which issue diplomas or certificates which are misleading with respect to the professional appointment allowing the practice of the profession.

Art. 14 – Sworn interpreters and translators may not use their titles and posts in the Association during their professional practice, except for those acts performed on its behalf.

Interprofessional behaviour

Art. 15 – Sworn interpreters and translators must abstain from performing voluntary acts or efforts to, in bad faith, gain other colleague's clients.

Art. 16 – Sworn interpreters and translators must act fully conscious of the feeling of professional solidarity. They must not formulate manifestations that might be detrimental for other colleague's suitability, prestige or ethics in the practice of the profession.

Publicity

Art. 17 – Any publicity offering professional services must be done in an honourable way.

Professional Secrecy

Art. 18 – The relationship between the professional and their client must develop under the fullest reserve and trust. Professionals must not publicize any matter without the express consent of their clients, nor use on their own benefit, or in that of third parties, the knowledge of the client's affairs, acquired as a result of their professional work.

Art. 19 – Sworn interpreters and translators are relieved from their duty of professional secrecy when they must indispensably reveal their knowledge for their own defence, to the extent that the information they reveal is indispensable.

Fees

Art. 20 – Sworn interpreters and translators must not agree fees that are substantially below those recommended by the Association.

Art. 21 – Sworn interpreters and translators must not accept shares or commissions for business which, in professional practice, are commissioned to other colleagues, except for those corresponding to the joint performance of a job or those arising from their membership in professional partnerships. Likewise, they will not accept commissions or shares for businesses, affairs or transactions, which, in relation to their professional activity, they facilitate to professionals of other professions or to third parties.

Conflict of interest

Art. 22 – Sworn interpreters and translators must not perform professional activity when they have any kind of interest which might conflict with those of their client, unless they have previously informed the client.

A common deontological principle for official translators is not to translate from or into any language for which they are not authorized.

In some countries like the United Kingdom it is generally considered contrary to the ethics of the profession to translate into a language other than the mother tongue of the translator. This position is clearly outdated and, in my opinion, should be changed. It has its base in principles exclusive to literary translation. Professional practice in other fields shows that translation into a non-mother tongue is needed (native professional translators are not always available, nor do clients usually assume the need for them) and this kind of translation can be done – and in fact is done – in compliance with the market quality requirements.

Many deontological rules overlap with common law rules and, in the end, they are used in order to protect members from ordinary courts and law. In my opinion, these coinciding rules (dealing with liabilities and damages derived from malpractice) should be abolished from the professional codes of ethics.

Some translators with strong ideological or political views feel inclined to make deontological principles out of their own beliefs (ethical principles) and consider that working for armies, law enforcing bodies, reactionary or conservative governments, criminals, multinational companies, confessional associations etc. violates what is 'respectable' (politically correct) for the profession. If applied, this interpretation would mean the imposition of personal beliefs on the overall members of a profession and would impede translators from working for most of the available sources of work. I think this position is unacceptable. Personal ethical principles should only be enforceable for the individual. This does not imply any contempt for professional ethics; it is simply an attempt to establish a clear separation between the personal and collective levels. At the same time, within each of us, the practice of official translation and personal ethics are inseparable; there are few other activities in which each problem and its solution entail such an ethical dilemma.

6.2.3 Traditions and customs

Most of the norms considered to be compulsory are, in fact, no more than uses and customs followed by a significant number of translators. These norms vary over time and according to the changing situations. Their obligatory status, if accepted, derives exclusively from their belonging to the way of translating expected by clients and recipients (default translation). They sustain a conservative way of translating that seeks to minimize risks for the translator and/or the translation. These kinds of rules are linked to literal translating, to the avoidance of deception and to the norms of format and style described in Section 7.2. They should not be taken as compulsory but just as a guide to what is safe and what is not at a given moment. They should be constantly adapted to times and situations, through their perpetual – and reasonable – adaptation. Our goal must be to translate increasingly better, not to translate the same way all the time, and, as a consequence of that, translate increasingly worse.

In addition to the rules for format and style, other norms are similarly based on uses and customs. They may involve translating only into the mother tongue, translating only from original documents, translating documents in full, not improving the style of the original, translating on official paper, the system of signing, stapling or signing and sealing both original and translation, etc.

6.2.4 Constraints imposed by the client, the initiator or the recipient

The translator's freedom is constrained not only by laws, professional regulations and uses and customs, but also by the constraints that other participants in the act of translation impose or try to impose.

For instance, clients and their representatives may try to impose favourable solutions (this should be rejected by the translator) or a special way of translating (mainly literally, as this is the commonly held concept of translation, which might be accepted by the translator). As we have seen, an extreme case is when clients bring an existing translation to the official translator and just request a validation. Apparently this is a profitable situation for some translators, but most professionals are clearly against it, for reasons analyzed above.

The recipient of the official translation is, mainly, the public authorities. As we have seen, they demand a very literal translation in order to minimize the risk of deception, but they do not know that literal translation is in many cases inadequate and in a significant number of cases unacceptable. The official translator should respect the demands from the authorities only if a violation is expected to invalidate the translation.

As already mentioned, there are other translation assignments for the official translator where the recipient is not an administrative body but a company;

this is the case in Spain with the bank La Caixa, which grants scholarships to study abroad. The documents presented by the applicant must be translated into English by a sworn translator and the bank supplies a compulsory table of grade equivalences to be followed. Even if you think the equivalences stipulated are not the most accurate or that the system itself is flawed, there is no way out: if the translation is to be accepted, you must abide by the stipulated equivalences. The translator's dilemmas are thus solved.

To summarize, one can describe hundreds of norms in official translation but not all of them should be considered strictly observable. There is tension in official translation between being adequate to professional quality standards and being acceptable to the public authorities, just as there is tension between the faithfulness and easy identification on the one hand, and style and plausibility on the other. Each translator has their own criteria for solving this dilemma and you should not expect uniform conclusions. Our advice would be to abide by as many norms as possible and transform your discarded norms into instruments available for when you need them.

6.3 Freedom

Although there are many views of the translation process, the translator usually has the choice to render a certain unit or segment in a number of different ways without affecting the validity of the translation. Practice and common sense show us every day that there is not just one adequate translation for a text, that those who look for the true translation in equivalence between languages are wrong. Translation is not an operation of comparing languages; it is a communicative and creative act.

There are some factors or parameters that lead us to reduce the number of translation choices we have. Some of these parameters concern the *macrotext*, others refer to the *microtext*. Once we have taken a choice on the macrotextual level, the choices for microtext are reduced as well, as there is a certain relationship between the two levels. This processing of information corresponds to a top-down process. However, if we notice any problem during the basic processing of the microtext (the default solutions adopted do not seem to work), then we shift to a bottom-up approach and look for other adequate solutions. Microtranslation choices concern the different means of expression (or ways to translate) available to the translator. All of them are open at the beginning; their number is reduced once we have decided the general way to translate the text and, occasionally, they widen again upon discovering a particular problem.

Factors that reduce the number of choices in translation (*translation constraints*) are:

- meaning constraints: both in source and target texts
- textual constraints: type, function, content (both in source and target texts)
- translation constraints: depending on the social situation of the act of translation, law and collegiate regulations, etc.
- ethical constraints at various levels
- communicative constraints: communicants, goal, vehicle, means and signals
- assignment constraints: deadlines, price, other mercantile considerations
- conceptual constraints: depending on the concept of translation held by the translator
- ability constraints: the translator's skills
- risk constraints: the risks assumed by the translator.

However, even when we have reduced the number of translation choices by applying all these constraints, the choices remain open. Factors that help widen the number of choices (*translation resources, translation variation*) are:

- variation in the target language (synonymy)
- need for solutions to new problems
- the concept of translation held by the translator
- the translator's skills
- personal creativity.

In the case of official translation, the social situation reduces the choices enormously. There are demands by recipients, clients and initiators, demands in each case derived from their interests, worries and beliefs about translation. To that must be added the pressure of ethical considerations, the legal regulations (if any), and the translator's awareness that official translation is a high-risk activity. All of this results in a default way of translating, a mode that is generally literal and conservative.

At the same time, however, a number of specific problems, common sense, the resources of language and our own creativity quite often lead us to transgress this default translation mode. We may do as much as we can in order to:

- improve the style and understanding of the translated text
  - omitting unnecessary text such as reiterations, references, formulae
  - increasing concision, precision, coherence, consistency
  - homogenizing terminology
  - correcting errors and mistakes
  - updating and neutralizing language
- make the text plausible
  - introducing specific elements recognizable as belonging to the target language and text
- provide cultural/institutional information and explanations when necessary

- avoid lexical and semantic gaps
- clarify meanings through our own interpretation within non-established limits
- facilitate the identification of references
- improve lay-out
- make the assignment as cheap as possible for the client
- satisfy our aesthetic, emotional, creative and professional impulses.

All these elements contribute to the freedom of the official translator and may produce a high number of different versions for the same meanings and the same text, all of them indistinguishable from the point of view of the validity or adequacy of the translation. As a matter of fact, two very similar renderings of the same text would seem suspicious; the same translator would translate in different ways at different moments. The norms of official translation (the ways in which the statistical majority of translators work) are constantly evolving. As with surgeons, translators can be more or less competent, and can adjust more or less to their clients' expectations and preferences.

Suggested activities

1) Look at the joint-venture contract in the Appendix. Now write another contract of the same kind, in English, with new details for new participants.
   The new data should concern Managing and Investing parties, place, date,
   duration, terms and conditions, distribution of benefits, etc.
2) Translate the same joint-venture contract with different goals:
   – to inform your client about its contents (on-sight translation with a tape
     recorder)
   – to inform your client about its contents (by writing an abridged version)
   – to be executed by both parties in their corresponding countries
   – to be executed by both parties in a foreign country (your own country), as
     if it had been generated at this country originally
   – as if it had been executed and was presented as evidence in a court of law
     (official)
   – to be included as an example of this kind of contract in a manual of inter-
     national mercantile law
   – as an exam
   – as a test for a job application.
3) Add new translation procedures of your own, in addition to those described
   in this chapter.
4) Translate the US death certificate in the Appendix in a way you think is
   absolutely acceptable for a judge in your country (complete, literal, etc.).
   Then translate the same certificate in a way that the judge would hesitate to
   accept.

5) Get a code of ethics current for official translators in your country (or the FIT one if no other is available). Assess the code according to your own convictions.

6) It is common practice nowadays for translation companies to ask the translator to make a critical assessment of a translation offered to a prospective client by another firm, with the aim of 'robbing' that client. Would you accept this job?

7) In chapter 3, all the members of your group gave different translations of the joint-venture contract in the Appendix. Underline and comment on those differences that affect neither the meaning nor the acceptability of the translation and merely reflect personal style and creativity. Try and evaluate those different personal styles of translating.

7. Common Problems and Frequent Solutions

7.1 Means of expression

Macrotext

If we return to Christiane Nord's distinction between *documental* and *instrumental* types of translation, we find that official translation would be included among the documental type, since "the target text, in this case, is a text about a text, or about one or more particular aspects of a text" (Nord 1997:47). To understand this, we need to recall that, even in cases in which the translated text is valued as an original, there always remains the need to allow the translated text to be compared to its original. The search for fidelity to the original is a need felt by the recipients of the translations (judges, administrators). It must thus be possible to compare this kind of translation to its original. Fidelity here is not easy to explain, as the hermeneutics of legal texts remain something of a mystery – a mixture of words (documents: the only material substance) and opinions (depending on the interests of the parties or the interpretation of different judges, often hidden or vague intentions and debatable rules of interpretation). If in literary translation the need to compare to the original implies fidelity to the author's words and intentions, in official translation this need derives from an imprecise, undefined fidelity to words, meanings and intentions, according to the set of rules for interpretation which constitute the law.

This distinction might be clearer if we think of two different ways of presenting translations:

- the *original-plus-translation type*: where both texts coexist and are subject to comparison
- the *translation-only-type*: where, as soon as the translation is written, the original (which can run from a real text that is being replicated to a text that inspired the target text) disappears and no further comparison is needed, possible or necessary.

Even when a legal text may be subject to both kinds of translation, the situation of official translation clearly corresponds to the original-plus-translation type.

A further distinction can be made (Mayoral and Muñoz 1997) between *focus on the source culture*:

Original	Translation	Back-translation
House of Representatives	Cámara de los Representantes	Chamber of Representatives

and *focus on the target culture*:

House of Representatives	equivalente del Congreso de los Diputados	the equivalent to the Spanish *Congreso de los Diputados*

This distinction overlaps, respectively, with that between *stress on identification*:

District Court	Juzgado de distrito	District Court

and *stress on understanding* (Mayoral and Muñoz 1997):

District Court	Juzgado de Primera Instancia	Court of First Instance

Such choices restrict the options for translation procedures at macro and microtextual levels.

At the *macrotextual* level, official translation follows the original text: changes in order, number of words and fidelity to the dictionary meaning of the original words are reduced to a reasonable minimum in order to favour easy identification:

- *exegetic procedures* are avoided
- *multiple procedures* are avoided
- *default solutions* are favoured
- *cognates* are used when useful for keeping an easy reference to the original words
- *errors in meaning* are kept
- *simplification* of the original when possible (doublets, triplets, synonyms, clumsy syntax meet with strong resistance).

All of this is justified by an intention to be literal and complete.

The demand for literalism and fidelity strongly favours translations that focus on the original culture and stress identification. This holds even when problems with understanding, style, plausibility, precision, economy, etc., cause focus and stress to shift. We may even resort to multiple and simultaneous ways of translating, quite often clearing the way for other specific solutions contradictory – or complementary – to these.

Microtext

Problems such as *validation procedures* are avoided, as they are not the translator's concern and may lead to biased translations. For example, official translators should *not* risk the following supposed equivalences:

Original	Translation	'Back-translation'
Bachelor of Arts	Licenciado en Filosofía y Letras	Degree in Philosophy and Letters (four or five years)
B+	Notable	Distinction

Translation procedures

In navigating between the macrotextual and microtextual levels, several translation procedures are routinely in evidence:

Cognates

Cognate strongly facilitate identification, so they are often used for the names of laws, courts, institutions or legal concepts that do not exist in the target culture:

Original	Translation
District Court	Corte/Tribunal de Distrito
Beneficio de excusión	Benefit of excussio

Borrowings

Borrowings or *loan words* are necessary when identification is the main concern, as is the case of proper nouns, degrees, grades, etc.:

Original	Translation
Bachelor of Arts	Bachelor of Arts
B+	B+

They are also necessary when, generally speaking, there is no equivalence between concepts in the two cultures:

Common Law	Common Law
Trust	Trust

But if the need to understand is added, *doublets* comprising borrowings plus *exegetic solutions* might be recommendable:

Bachelor of Arts	Bachelor Arts [first three-or four-year university degree]

Calques

Calques are useful when we lack adequate terms in the target language. However, they quite often interfere with understanding when the concepts are not equivalent and the convenience of further procedures should be considered:

Original	Translation	Back-translation
with First Class honours	con honores de primera clase (la calificación más alta)	with honours of the First Class (the highest attainable mark)
severability	separabilidad (condición de un contrato que permite la anulación parcial de sus cláusulas)	status that allows some parts only of a contract to be annulled
equity	equidad (sistema jurídico anglosajón que recurre a los principios generales del derecho)	English legal system based on the general principles of law

There are also cases where calques pose no further problems:

Registration District	Distrito de Registro	Registration District

Omission

Omission is quite dangerous as a solution for official translation but might be reasonable in certain cases when the information included in the original is no longer relevant (see section 4.2 above). In the case of formulaic expressions, empty of meaning and which have no literal translation, it can become a convenient solution:

Original	Translation
PROVIDED HOWEVER THAT	∅
NOW THEREFORE	∅

Simplification

Simplification of the original can be seen as a special case of omission, and may turn out to be quite recommendable, particularly when translating from English. The abuse of doublets, triplets, reiterations, multi-particle references, etc. makes translation from English into other languages quite often unpalatable and unreadable, and the meaning is already present, implicitly or expressly, in the texts. For example:

Synonyms

Original	Translation	Back-translation
transfer and assign	transferir	transfer
authorizations, approvals and consents	autorizaciones	authorizations

Occasionally, the opposite procedure is advisable, due to characteristics of the languages involved:

Original	Translation	Back-translation
If any action is taken against this Joint Venture, individually or severally, as a result of actions taken or agreements entered into by this Joint Venture	En caso de emprenderse acciones legales contra esta Empresa Conjunta, de forma individual o colectiva, por actuaciones desarrolladas o acuerdos suscritos por esta Empresa Conjunta	If any legal action is taken against this Joint Venture, individually or severally, as a result of actions taken or agreements entered into by this Joint Venture

Aggregation of several meanings into one

'Aggregate translations' consist of the use of a simple solution for a complex meaning, using as few words as possible in a way that collects all the different meanings of the original in a global way. It makes understanding of the translation much easier and the text much more readable but can suppress the explicitness intended in the original, when the author expressly wishes to state some individual case. The resulting contraction of text might also seem suspicious to many recipients. It should therefore be used with the utmost discretion in official translation.

Due to a lack of equivalence:

Original	Translation	Back-translation
Tribunal and Courts	Tribunales	Courts [without distinction]
Common law or equity	Ley	Law [without distinction between systems]
waive demand, presentment for payment, protest, notice of protest, and notice of non-payment	renuncia a los derechos que le correspondan en relación con plazos y trámites	waive their right to stipulated periods and procedures
provision of law, statute, rule, regulation	normas legales	legal norms
order, judgement, decree	resolución judicial	judicial resolution

Due to considerations of style:

Original	Translation	Back-translation
books, records, accounts, documentations or other information	toda información	all information

But this is subject to the possible intention expressly to mention all the different elements:

books, records, accounts, documentations or other information	libros de contabilidad, registros, cuentas, documentos u otra información	books, records, accounts, documentation or other information

Multiparticles:

Multiparticles of various kinds may often be omitted:

hereby	ø	ø
covering Loss hereunder	que cubra la pérdida	covering loss

Reiteration:

Implicit or obvious information may also be omitted:

which constitute any part of the Loan between the Obligee and Principal	que forme parte del préstamo	which constitute part of the Loan

Multiplication

Despite the multiplicity of simplification strategies, the characteristics of the target language may make the inverse procedure, multiplication, very useful:

Original	Translation	Back-translation
agrees	pacta y conviene	accords and convenes
encumbrances	cargas y gravámenes	charges and encumbrances

Functional adaptation

In the absence of direct equivalents, the translator may use the concept that performs approximately the same function in the target language:

District Court	Juzgado de Primera Instancia	Court of First Instance

The literal meaning might be also replaced by the function that the person performs in the source culture:

solicitor	notario	notary public
Assistant Manager	apoderado	authorised signatory, attorney for the Bank

However, this kind of procedure is not always advisable in official translation.

Linguistic adaptation

Sometimes the translator adapts the expression to terms and phrases that are natural in the target language:

Changing grammatical person

For instance, first persons may become third persons, in accordance with target norms:

Original	Translation	Back-translation
I do hereby certify that	el abajo firmante certifica que	the undersigned certifies that
I appoint	el Otorgante designa	the Principal appoints

Exchanging formulaic elements

Source-culture formulas may be rendered by corresponding formulas in the target culture:

Original	Translation	Back-translation
IN WITNESS WHEREOF the parties hereto have set their hands hereunder	Y en prueba de conformidad y aceptación firman el presente	And as a proof of conformity and acceptance, they sign the present document

Omitting upper-case letters

Stylistic norms may also require modification of capitalization:

Original	Translation	Back-translation
the Seller	el vendedor	the seller

More generally, the translator may choose to follow the text conventions of the target language (see section 8.3).

Approximate solutions

When no equivalence is found between languages and systems, solutions approaching the meaning of the original may be enough, even when this is not the optimal solution:

Original	Translation	Back-translation
trust	fideicomiso	fidei-commisum
Federal expense	gasto público	public expense
Registry of Births and Deaths	Registro Civil	Civil Registry
Office of Vital Statistics	Registro Civil	Civil Registry
non-circumvention and non-disclosure	confidencialidad	confidentiality
Registrar	Secretario General	General Secretary

Generalization

Generalization may provide useful solutions when there is a lack of equivalence:

Original	Translation	Back-translation
deed	documento	document
attorney-in-law	abogado	lawyer

Unification

When the same party is named in different ways in the same document, we can choose to unify these denominations into just one:

Original	Translation	Back-translation
Principal, Obligor, Borrower, Debtor, Guarantee, Insured	prestatario	borrower

Personification

This is the solution in cases where the target language does not allow legal acts to be personalized as English does:

Original	Translation	Back-translation
a corresponding credit facility is willing to proceed with the funding of the project	el Prestamista está dispuesto a financiar el proyecto	the Lender is willing to proceed with the funding of the project
the Guarantee shall pay to the Obligee	el Avalista pagará al Obligante	the Guarantor shall pay to the Obligee

Ex novo creations

'Ex novo' neologisms are purely invented words. They are not advisable in official translation as they facilitate neither identification nor understanding.

Fossilized translations

A concept common among official translators of Arabic and not so familiar to other translators is that of 'fossilized translation' (*patrón de traducción*) (Feria 2002a, Feria *et al.* 2002, Peña 1999). I find this concept quite useful to understand and explain some aspects of translating between culturally distant languages or languages that have been exposed to the activity of translation for a very long time, as is the case for Arabic and Spanish.

Translation conventions are defined as very old, traditional, purely conventional translation solutions for some concepts. They are used by most of the translators in a particular field and correspond to social, legal or administrative situations already forgotten. These translation solutions could be considered as canons or conventions at microtext level.

Many official translators render the Arabic *talaq* as *divorce*, although it means *repudiation*. 'Divorce' benefits the Western local authority, which thus avoids the dilemma of validating a legal act, repudiation, that may be unconstitutional and against the local law. This solution is inaccurate but convenient.

The Arabic *sadaq* is regularly translated as *dowry*. But the dowry (in fact, *shiwar*) is offered to the bride by her father as a custom whereas the *sadaq* is offered by the bridegroom as an element necessary for the legal validity of the marriage. This is usually low-risk information but could become critical. For instance, it could lead to the annulment of the marriage by a Spanish judge applying Moroccan law.

The Arabic *la ilaha illa Allah* is usually translated into Spanish as *No hay más dios que Dios* [*There is no god other than God*], which sounds quite strange. It might be more adequate to translate it as *Sólo hay un Dios* [*There is only one God*] or *Sólo Dios merece ser adorado* [*Only God deserves to be adored*]. The Arabic *bismi Allahi arrahmani arrahim* is a marker for the beginning of a speech; it is currently translated into Spanish as *En el nombre de Dios, el Compasivo, el Misericordioso* [*In the name of God, compassionate and merciful*]; it used to be translated as *In nomine Dei* or *En el nombre de Dios, piadoso de la piedad* [*In the name of God, merciful of mercy*].

The translator's dilemma is whether to be loyal to the translation conventions, which avoid responsibilities but are not immutable, or to be loyal to truth and ethics. Some translators from Arabic are not fully familiar with Islamic law, but they know the translation conventions (which, by the way, is what most of their recipients know). In this sense, translation conventions are shortcuts used to circumvent meaning.

Surrender

When the translator fails to find the meaning of a part of a document, as a lesser evil they may resort to the transcription of the original segment, abandoning their search for a better solution, losing that meaning and adding an oddity. This is a common occurrence with abbreviations that the translator cannot decipher due to a lack of adequate sources (scarcity of specialized dictionaries) or because the abbreviation has been created *ex novo*. When different writing systems intervene in translation, this solution takes the form of transliteration or phonetic transcription.

Correction

Errors with respect to facts should be treated with common sense, as we can find many different kinds of them: relevant/irrelevant, sensitive/indifferent to the interests of the parties, clear/unclear. On occasions they should be reflected literally but on other occasions this would not contribute anything positive to the translated text and they should be corrected or improved.

Stylistic and grammatical errors, in my opinion, should be corrected, without any further mention.

We move now to some general considerations of the above procedures.

Acceptability of non-literal translations

Some official translation cultures (in the US and Argentina for instance) show a radical rejection of strategies leading to non-literal, incomplete translations. Many of our suggestions here may be strongly opposed by them. A telling commentary is the slogan widely circulating among legal translators in the US: *Garbage in, garbage out,* meaning "we must reproduce whatever we are given, and we cannot just say 'This is a bunch of garbage, so pay no attention except to this part'". Other translation cultures have a more open attitude toward these strategies and procedures.

Titles or heads

Articles or clauses in English contracts and undertakings are usually preceded by titles that try to condense its meaning. But this is not the case for other languages. When a language, such as Spanish, does not use titles regularly in obligations, we are in trouble, since equivalents are not easily found. Faced with this situation, the translation of titles in official translation becomes the same as with other kinds of translation: you must resume, condense and keep only the essential meaning of the whole text. It quite often causes versions that stray a long way from the literal translation:

Original	Translation	Back-translation
Loan Servicing	Buena fe por parte del Prestatario y el Prestamista	Good faith on the part of the Borrower and the Lender

Units of translation

One of the main characteristics of legal texts is that they quite often present formulaic units of meaning that are called clauses, articles, stipulations, terms, conditions, etc. These may be represented in many ways, ranging from quite simple to quite complicated forms. For instance, the clause "other interests held cover" may be abbreviated as 'h/c', or it may be elaborated as "the insurance of other interests is pending additional payment".

We thus find numerous short forms that actually represent longer units of translation. The most representative abbreviations are the INCOTERMS, a set of international rules published by the International Chamber of Commerce, voluntarily accepted by the parties, that determine the construction of the commercial clauses included in an international agreement. The rules or clauses are expressed through very short phrases or initialisms. For example, 'FOB' stands for 'Free on board'. There are simple formulas that represent a full clause of almost 200 words, and which could be supplemented by an interpretation covering several pages. On other occasions (see section 8.3), several formulations convey the same meaning but use very different words.

All this suggests the translator should think about replacing complex clauses with simpler or clearer ones conveying the same meaning, even when many translators, clients and recipients find this kind of solution unacceptable for official translation. As a technical way of dealing with obtuse clauses, it might be sometimes advisable to reduce the clause to its minimum expression and later on add all the details of meaning present in the original which we find relevant and, therefore, impossible to omit.

This leads me to consider the possibility of considering the clause as a unit of translation in such cases.

The translator's marked presence

The need to be accurate, faithful, and to avoid forgery, etc. leads the official translator to intrude in the original text and, when appropriate or necessary, to intervene in the translation. All such intrusions are marked by the use of square brackets. This kind of interference on the part of the translator is characteristic of official translation and is not so acceptable for other kinds of translation. The need to certify their own work enhances the self-awareness of official translators. But they always do their best to make their commentaries perfectly distinguishable from what is included in the original text.

Sometimes the translator's intrusion reflects only their imperfect understanding of the original. That is the case, for instance, with the appearance of the commentary 'illegible'. Damage to a document may imply the risk of a loss of meaning due to physical conditions or to the lack of familiarity of the translator with the handwriting of the original text.

In the following sections we will review the procedures available for solving common problems in the translation of particular kinds of documents (see chapters 7 and 8).

7.2   Format and typing conventions

Format (or layout) is one of the elements that help transmit the global meaning of a text. It is commonly linked to the text type, especially with the popular categorization of legal texts. A text that conforms to an expected format is perceived as natural and plausible; if not, it is perceived as unnatural and manipulated.

The expected format for a certain text may be imposed either by law (for instance, the bill of exchange in Spain) or by custom (as in most cases). In the latter case, formats are not an absolute norm and a large degree of variation is permitted.

Let us see the traditional systems for converting a fully formatted original text into an affordable and faithful text.

7.2.1   Belonging to the original vs. belonging to the translation

In official translation, as in other kinds of translation, we have the convention that everything included between square brackets [ ] belongs to the translator and not to the source text. We thus find inserted texts such as the following:

> *[illegible signature], [blank], [original interrupted], [a word has been erased and a new word has been written instead], [grammatically incorrect, I think it meant to say "...."]*

Sometimes such text includes implicit information:

> Brighton [United Kingdom]

Generally speaking, an official translation has the following parts:

- translator's opening words (first part of their certification) [if the case may be]
- body of the document
- translator's closing words (second part of their certification)

- legalization of the translation by the applicable body [sometimes optional]
- international legalization of the above [Hague Apostille, ministry of foreign affairs and/or embassies in the foreign country] [optional if the prime legalization is optional].

Since the work of the translator ends with their closing statement, we need to separate the document itself from that certification. This can be achieved in a number of ways:

> **Opening formulas**
> Document
> **Closing formulas**

or

> Opening formulas
> "Document"
> Closing formulas

or both systems together:

> **Opening formulas**
> "Document"
> **Closing formulas**

Sometimes we add inverted commas before each line of the document:

> **Opening formulas**
> "line 1
> "line 2
> --------
> "line n
> **Closing formulas**

or even at the end of each line as well:

> **Opening formulas**
> "line 1"
> "line 2"
> --------
> "line n"
> **Closing formulas**

We usually use larger spacing to make separation clearer. But all these procedures are optional and of a very personal choice.

On other occasions, other comments by the translator are also included:

Opening formulas
Document
Affixed to this document there is an apostille, which says/Annexed to the former document, there is a ...., which says:
Apostille
This translation consists of three pages, all of which are signed and sealed.
Closing formulas

Sometimes a double certification by the translator is needed, for example with the translation of documents into foreign languages. In this case you might need, according to law, a certification written in the local language, which the local authorities can accept, and a second one written in the language of the translation, which can be read by the foreign authorities which receive the official translation. The translator should sign both certifications.

7.2.2 Converting complex formats into paragraph sequences

Consecutive order

The use of consecutive order consists in regrouping information into clusters that become separate paragraphs in the translation. The clusters are put in a consecutive order, which may be open to personal interpretations. The order ideally follows the natural order for reading in the source language (for Western languages, from left to right and top-down) and, if appropriate, chronological order as well. An exception is usually made for the name of the document (for instance, certified copy of an entry of birth), which we try to locate at the very beginning for the sake of clarity. As an example, let us see a fragment of a British birth certificate:

TRANSLATION CASE
Original text
(See Appendix)

Translated text

Certified Copy of an Entry of Birth
Pursuant to the Births and Deaths Registration Act 1953

B.C/R.B.D.

DQ 311756

The Statutory fee for this certificate is 3s. 9d. Where a search is necessary to find the entry, a search fee is payable in addition.

Registration District Haringey.- Birth in the Sub-district of Hornsey in the London Borough of Haringey.

1968

Column 1.– No.: 248.

Column 2.– When and where born: Eighth June 1968.– 31 Alexandra Park Road.

Column 2.– Name, if any: Linda Anne.

Column 3.– Sex: girl.

Column 4: Name and surname of father: ------.

Column 5.– Name, surname and maiden name of mother: ------------, formerly ------ -------, of 23 ------- Hornsey.

Column 6.– Occupation of father: Café proprietor.

Column 7.– Signature, description and residence of informant: -------------, brother .

Column 8.– When registered: Twelfth June 1968.

Column 9.– Signature of registrar: ----------------, Registrar.

Column 10.– Name entered after registration: ----------------

I, --------------, Registrar of Births and Deaths for the Sub-district of Hornsey, in the London Borough of Haringey do hereby certify that this is a true copy of the entry No. 248 in the Register of Births for the said Sub-district, and that such Register is now legally in my custody. Witness my hand this 13th day of June, 1968.- [Signed], Registrar of Births and Deaths.

CAUTION: Any person who (1) falsifies any of the Particulars on this certificate, or (2) uses a falsified certificate as true, knowing it to be false, is liable to prosecution.

As you can see, certain decisions taken have been taken with respect to punctuation:

- The sign ".–" (full stop plus dash), which is rare in regular writing practice, is used to separate parts of the text that are just separated by a blank in the original;
- The contents of the boxes are closed with a full stop, which does not exist in the original; it might as well have been closed without any punctuation marks.

Tables

A system similar to the columns above can be used for marks organized as tables in an academic transcript:

TRANSLATION CASE
Original Text

Dept	Course	Title of course	Units	Grade	Points
Fall 1979 Term Avg. 2.075					
Chem.	100	Fundamental Chemistry I	1.000	D	1.000
Por-Sc.	100	Academic Writing	1.000	C+	2.300
Eng.	105	20th Century Am	1.000	C	2.000
Span.	260	Literature	1.000	B	3.000
		Intro to Sp Am. Lit.			

UP 8.000   Grp. 16.900   4.000   8.300

Cum. Avg. 2.112

Translated Text

Fall 1979. – Term Average: 2.075
Department: Chemistry. – Course: 100. – Title of course: Fundamental Chemistry I.
– Units: 1.000. – Grade: D. – Points: 1.000
Porter-Scholar Program. – 100. – Academic Writing. – 1.000. – C+.– 2.300
English.- 105. – 20th Century American Literature. – 1.000. – C. – 2.000
Spanish. – 260. – Introduction to Spanish American Literature. – 1.000. – B. – 3.000
Term units: 4.000. – Term Points: 8.300. –Total units achieved: 8.000. –Cumulative
grade point: 16.900. – Cumulative Average: 2.112.

Here the headings are applied only to the first data, after which only data are
expressed in a consecutive way.

An intermediate system would be:

Fall 1979.– Term Average: 2.075
Department.– Course.– Title of course.– Units.– Grade.– Points
Chemistry.– 100.– Fundamental Chemistry I.– 1.000.– D.– 1.000
Porter-Scholar Program.– 100.– Academic Writing.– 1.000.– C+.– 2.300
English.– 105.– 20th Century American Literature.– 1.000.– C.– 2.000
Spanish.– 260.– Introduction to Spanish American Literature.– 1.000.– B.– 3.000
Term units: 4.000.– Term Points: 8.300.– Total units achieved: 8.000.– Cumulative
grade point: 16.900.– Cumulative Average: 2.112.

The Argentine society of sworn translators, for example, acknowledges
different types of text (like, for example, balance sheets) that are translated with the original format, layout or diagram.

Abbreviations

As can be seen above and in the preceding bill of exchange, it is common for
documents to be forms, with boxes and tables. This kind of organization imposes

serious spatial constraints and quite often words are used in a contracted, shortened way. This contracted use of words is sometimes an established form that
you can find in dictionaries. But quite often they are not established; they are
just invented by the writer trying to include a long piece of information in too
small a space. In translation, we usually do not have the same spatial constraints
as the original writers did, so it would not be reasonable to translate contracted
forms as contracted forms. We usually choose to translate the full forms of words
and phrases.

Chronological order

Sometimes we find different pieces of information in a document that can hardly
be subject to consecutive reading order. These include stamps, seals, signatures
and dates. Seals and stamps can appear anywhere and we do not usually interrupt a word or phrase to indicate that a stamp has been added. The same thing
occurs with the different elements in a single certification. Sometimes it is hard
to associate them just on the basis of their position in the documents.

In this situation, we can help the recipients of the translation by regrouping
the loose elements in an orderly, chronological way. For example, in a Pakistani
parental authorization to marry, we find the following in a natural reading order:

TRANSLATION CASE
Original Text

- raised seal of the Pakistan Ministry of Foreign Affairs
- an attestation signed by the Chief of Protocol of the Pakistan Ministry
  of Foreign Affairs in Lahore [inside the main body of text]
- certified and attested to be an exact translation of Urdu into English
- signature
- 25 January 1993 [inside the main body of text]
- attested
- deponent
- thumb print
- (L.T.I)
- seal of the notary with signature and date
- (Abdul Kareem) (Father)
- signature
- seal of the Chairman of Town Committee
- seal and signature of a Magistrate
- seal of the Town Committee
- attestation Stamp with ink stamp of the Pakistan Ministry of Foreign
  Affairs

Translated Text
Immediately after the name of the document (Affidavit), we would include

Certified and attested to be exact translation of Urdu into English. –
[Signature]

Immediately after the main body of the text, we would add:

Deponent. – Abdul Kareem, father. – [Thumb impression]. – Left thumb
impression.
Attested. – [Seal of the notary]. – [Signed]. – Date
[Seal and signature of the Magistrate]
[Seal of the Chairman of Town Committee]
[Attestation stamp and ink stamp of the Pakistan Ministry of Foreign
Affairs]
Attestation of the Chief of Protocol of the Pakistan Ministry of Foreign
Affairs. – [Signature]. – 25 January 1993. – [Raised seal of the Pakistan
Ministry of Foreign Affairs]

7.2.3   Text vs. image

Traditionally the official translator must reflect everything the original document shows. This mainly applies to text (be it handwritten or typewritten),
drawings, signatures (legible or illegible), letterheads, stamps and seals, eras-
ures and alterations, interruptions in the original, etc. Everything different from
pure legible text is usually expressed between brackets. But the borders are not
always clear.

Sometimes letterheads are not rendered unless they contribute new information (name of a company or body, address). If reflected, they should only refer
to the information contained and not the fact that they are letterheads.

Many forms are completed by hand, and there is no need to reflect this fact
with any translator's comment.

Quite often signatures are systematically rendered as 'illegible' by the translator, even when some of them may be legible. This is to avoid all risk of making
mistakes.

Sometimes stamps are treated as pure text, without any indication of their
nature as stamps (this is mainly in the case of legalization stamps).

Seals and stamps

Seals and stamps are usually rendered inside brackets (with the exception just
mentioned of legalization stamps). Their description can be either exhaustive or
simple. A quite detailed translation of a stamp could read:

[Round	red	ink	seal	which reads "……………"]
[Rectangular	purple	raised	stamp	of ………..]
[Triangular		green		

A *raised* or *embossed seal* is made with a machine that impresses the relief or embossment of the seal without any ink. You should be cautious about them because they are not legible in photocopies and faxes. If you accept photocopies or faxes to translate you should check to see if the original has any seals of this kind.

Not all the particulars in the former model of translation for a seal are always used.

The translator is not liable for the authenticity of the seals and stamps. Just translating them is enough. Cautions on translating the seals and stamps are thus usually unnecessary, even when, in cases where you are suspicious about the authenticity of a seal or stamp, you might choose the formula "which reads"/ "which states that it belongs to", as opposed to more straightforward formulas such as "of".

The use of seals and stamps may differ from one country to another. In Spain, you cannot imagine an official document without its corresponding seal; any recipient would feel suspicious in the absence of a seal. But in other cases, like the United Kingdom, many documents coming from administrative bodies do not bear a seal.

7.2.4   Avoiding deception

Whenever somebody wants something from a public authority, a suspicion of deception arises. Whenever there is an agreement or controversy between different parties, a suspicion of deception arises. Whenever a translator is paid by a claimant or a party, a suspicion of deception is cast upon the translator and the translator may feel the same position with respect to their client. Fear of deception is the main reason – together with a lack of knowledge about translation – why the recipients of official translations demand literal (true and faithful) translations.

The Argentine society of sworn translators states that the translator should accept that the original is "complete, cannot be modified, and is irreplaceable, both in its totality and in part".

At this point we are mentioning only some of the reasons why a translator might be suspicious of their client (for further information, see Section 3.2, Loyalties). This suspicion is embodied in an ethical principle:

> The official translator should always translate from original documents
> and never from photocopies or copies coming through fax.

This principle is not applied on many occasions, when the trust of the translator in their client is strong enough. The translator thus takes on a risk.

Photocopies produce a loss in legibility with respect to the original and increase the risk of manipulation. If the client presents a photocopy, we should ask to check the original; once checked, we can translate the photocopy as if it were an original. If the client does not present the original, we should advise them that the fact that it is a photocopy will be mentioned in our translation. Interruptions and illegibility in the original will be also reflected in our translation. Sometimes the original is unavailable and one has to translate from a non-original copy. In such cases the translator disclaims liability by making it clear in their certification that they have translated 'a photocopy' or 'a fax' of an original document. If our trust in the client is strong because we know them well, or if they are an administrative body, an ONG, a translation company (entities not usually suspected of deception), or if the information in the document is not particularly sensitive (description of a course, primary education certificate), we sometimes accept photocopies as originals, at our own risk.

One way of manipulating the contents of a document is by translating only fragments of it in order to dilute the context, thus permitting interpretations different to those originally intended. In some cases, the translation must be of the *full* document and a fragmentary translation is theoretically barred. But it stands to reason that on other occasions a full translation is not advisable (think of a student or graduate who only needs the syllabi of six courses contained in a university handbook). In these cases, the translator will render only the relevant fragments but will try to make it clear in their certification that they have translated 'fragments' of an original. The Argentine society prescribes the use of the formula "This is a partial translation of the annexed document, of its pages xxx to xxxx". It also establishes the need for the translator to state if any element "considered unnecessary by the client" has been omitted.

Generally speaking, a translator must read the original carefully, searching for possible falsifications or alterations. If falsifications or alterations are found and the translator thinks they must reflect them in the translation, the translator should inform the client about this prior to accepting the job.

Some aspects of traditional formats for official translation are derived from this effort to avoid deception. To avoid the translation being manipulated after it has been delivered to the client, the official translator has traditionally (and exclusively depending on their own choice and preferences) used the following procedures:

- not leaving any blank spaces in the lines
- left-justifying all lines
- suppressing interparagraph blanks
- adding inverted commas.

For example:

"I do hereby certify that the following particulars are true ----------------------------
"I do hereby certify that the following particulars are true ……………………............

"I do hereby certify that the following particulars are true ..../-
"Birth certificate ....
"Birth certificate ...."

The Argentine society states that "[t]he text of the translation should not contain blanks, filling them with dashes". This kind of procedure has largely disappeared with the use of computers.

One of the concerns of recipients is that the translation may not have a corresponding original. In principle, the official translation should in many cases be accorded the same status as a true and original document. But there are cases in which judges and officials take additional precautions, demanding not only that the original be presented together with the translation, but that the original be attached to the translation in one way or another (sometimes by staples) and that both documents share the seal, signature and even the certification of the translator. This requirement mostly cannot be met because no client is willing to allow the translator to alter a diploma or an identification document such as a passport. It is advisable to negotiate with the recipient in these cases. An intermediate solution may be to attach a certified photocopy to the translated text. The Argentine society states that "[t]he original instrument must accompany and precede the translation" and, if this is impossible, the fact should be stated and certified by the translator.

7.2.5   One source language

Official translators are authorized for specific languages; they may not translate from just any language to any other language. If they translate between non-authorized languages, their translations will probably be declared null and void, and the translator will be causing harm to their clients. A translator should state in their certification the language or languages for which they are authorized to translate.

If an English document includes something in a different language, that third language should be kept in the translation. There are many borderline cases however:

- As already mentioned in Section 3.4, in Pakistani documents written in English or translated into this language you always find many Urdu words and some Arabic ones. In order to make the translation understandable, you must translate the Urdu words, considering these Urdu words as a part of Pakistani English.
- The Hague legalizations written in English usually contain the following words in French "APOSTILLE (Convention de La Haye du 5 octobre 1961)". I always transgress my attributions and translate those words into English: no harm intended and no harm done.

- An Irish birth certificate states "Clárlann Breitheanna Agus Básanna", and no English meaning is given for the Gaelic, which means "Registry of Births and Deaths". If you are reasonably certain about the meaning, translating helps understanding and identification, even though you are not an official translator for Gaelic.

The Argentine society requires the formula "The original document contains third-language expressions, which have not been translated".

7.2.6 Legibility

In some kinds of translation we are entitled to guess what an illegible fragment means and to translate it accordingly. This is not the case in official translation. Everything illegible should be rendered as "[illegible]".

An especial case of illegibility is that of *handwritten texts*. There are many difficulties in reading handwriting from different languages and traditions. Consultation with the client and/or other speakers of the language is usually necessary. Remember to read the whole handwritten text and consult the client on accepting the job. Also remember to ask how to contact the client quickly in case any hesitation arises during the translation.

Signatures are a very special case of handwriting, so special that we reproduce most of them as "[illegible]" so as to avoid making a mistake.

7.2.7 Understandability

Even when you master a foreign language, you can always find certain parts that you cannot understand. The reasons may be:

- the writer had a problem expressing themselves
- the writer has introduced unintended ambiguity
- the writer has introduced intended ambiguity
- there are typewriting or editing errata
- the original text is damaged
- the source language is not the writer's mother tongue
- the writer is used to a writing system different to that used in the document.

Usually we do not introduce any comment on this kind of problem; we just 'improve' the original. But if the error could have consequences for any of the parties, we should try to ensure that our translation makes clear what has happened and we should not attempt 'improvement'.

The translator's mandate to interpret the text nevertheless has highly subjective limits. Conservative translators (who do not dare to risk making a mistake) opt for conservative solutions (no interpretation at all); more daring translators tend to elaborate the original, although not to the extent of affecting anyone's rights. In Section 3.4 we mentioned some typical problems with the written English in Pakistani documents. Consultation with native speakers always makes things easier in this respect.

7.2.8   Originality

Demanding the original documents is not only a guarantee against illegibility. As we have mentioned, it is also a guarantee against deception, as alterations and falsifications are much more difficult to discover in a photocopy or fax that in an original.

However, despite the major risks involved, the transmission of source documents by fax or the Internet is placing increasing pressure on translators to work without the original, and there is increasing acceptance of these conditions by official translators.

7.2.9   Other writing conventions

Uppercase letters

Some original texts are written in uppercase letters:

FOR VALUE RECEIVED, THE MAKER, BY THIS LOAN NOTE ("THE NOTE") UNCONDITIONALLY AND IRREVOCABLY PROMISES TO PAY TO .... GIBRALTAR, OR ANY SUBSEQUENT ASSIGNEE OF THE NOTE (BOTH HEREINAFTER CALLED "THE PAYEE") THE AMOUNT OF GBP 500,000 (FIVE HUNDRED THOUSAND POUNDS STERLING)

Unless the brief states otherwise, the translator usually converts this into a regular text, with upper and lowercase letters (not always with the same result for different translators):

For value received, the Maker, by this Loan Note ("the Note") unconditionally and irrevocably promises to pay to ...... Gibraltar, or any subsequent assignee of the Note (both hereinafter called "the Payee") the amount of GBP 500,000 (Five Hundred Thousand Pounds Sterling)

Markers of emphasis

There are several markers of emphasis: size, fonts, upper case, small capitals, italics, bold face, underlining, different kinds of justification and centring, either individually or in combination. In the texts subject to official translation, they usually help to organize the text, indicating the different levels of its structure. But we can also find markers of emphasis used just for the sake of emphasis:

The Escrow Agent will <u>NOT</u> accept non-certified funds
The Escrow Agent <u>MUST</u> follow the conditions
Has been instructed to transfer said funds <u>without further authorization</u> in accordance with the terms and conditions

Unless the brief expressly states otherwise, the translator must not feel obliged to reproduce the elements of emphasis contained in the original. They can just choose among those available, in the same way as they are not obliged to reproduce tables, boxes, schemes and other structural elements of the original texts. Nor do I think it necessary to reproduce the 'emphasis for the sake of emphasis' markers just described. All such markers are more powerful than needed for the goal intended.

7.2.10 Translating into different formats

Texts of the same kind may and often do present different formats (i.e. bills of exchange or agreements). Occasionally the same document can be translated in different ways:

TRANSLATION CASE
1) Original text
No. CP/13/92   Singapore, 14/5/92
At 30 days sight of this first Bill of Exchange (second unpaid), pay to the order of Exporter's Bank
the sum of United States dollars: sixteen thousand and thirty five cents only (US$16,000.35)
for value received drawn under D/P at 30 days sight against shipt of our inv. CP/13/92 as per AWB No. 217-5332-7341 (HAWB 19712) on 13/5/92 through Importer's Bank for A/C of Importer.
Importer's Bank   Name and address of the Drawer
I accept: [Seal of Importer's Bank]
Pay to the order of Importer's Bank. Value for collection. For Exporter's Bank. [signed]. [Seal of Exporter's Bank]

2) Translated text strictly following the original
No. CP/13/92   Singapore, 14/5/92
At 30 days sight of this first Bill of Exchange (second unpaid), pay to the order of Exporter's Bank
the sum of United States dollars: sixteen thousand and thirty five cents only (US$16,000.35)
for value received drawn under documents against payment at 30 days sight against

shipment of our invoice CP/13/92 as Air Waybill No. 217-5332-7341 (House Air Waybill 19712) on 13/5/92 through Importer's Bank for account of Importer.
Importer's Bank   Name and address of the Drawer
I accept: [Seal of Importer's Bank]
Pay to the order of Importer's Bank. Value for collection. For Exporter's Bank.
[signed]. [Seal of Exporter's Bank]

3) Translated text following the original order
No. CP/13/93   Singapore, 14/5/92
At 30 days sight of this first Bill of Exchange (second unpaid), pay to the order of Exporter's Bank
the sum of United States dollars: sixteen thousand and thirty five cents (US$16,000.35) for value received drawn under documents against payment at 30 days sight against shipment of our invoice CP/13/92 as per Air Waybill No. 217-5332-7341 (House Air Waybill 19712) on 13/5/92 through Importer's Bank for account of Importer.
Name and address of the Drawee: Importer's Bank
Name and address of the Drawer: The Exporter
I accept: [Seal of Importer's Bank]
Endorsement: [Seal of Exporter's Bank]. Pay to the order of Importer's Bank. Value for collection. For Exporter's Bank. [Signed]

4) Translated text not following the original order (following the standard target language format)
No. CP/13/93
Drawing place: Singapore   Amount: USD 16,000.35
Drawing date: 14/5/92   Due date: 30 days sight
For this first BILL OF EXCHANGE (second unpaid) you will pay at the expressed maturity to the order of Exporter's Bank the amount of United States dollars sixteen thousand and thirty five cents.
Clauses: drawn under documents against payment at 30 days sight against shipment of our invoice CP/13/92 as per Air Waybill No. 217-5332-7341 (House Air Waybill 19712) on 13/5/92 through Importer's Bank for account of Importer.
Name and address of Drawee: Importer's Bank   Signature, name and address of the Drawer: The Exporter
I accept, on ....: [Seal of Importer's Bank]
By guarantee of [blank]   Pay to the order of Importer's Bank. Value for collection. Name and address of Endorser: For Exporter's Bank. [Signed]

Choosing between one format and another can depend on many different factors; sometimes it ultimately depends on the translator's wishes or inclination. In most cases, neither law nor associative norms provide a clear basis. The law usually says no more than that the official translation must be 'true and faithful'. For most recipients and clients, this means the official translation must be as literal as possible, following the original's format, information and order.

This situation makes it almost impossible to use system (4); it strongly leans towards systems (2) and (3).

To respect the format fully would mean reproducing the position of information within the text, the different fonts, sizes, means of highlighting (underlining, black, italics, boxes, etc.). This has traditionally been considered too demanding for the attainable results. Nevertheless, the use of computers has offered new possibilities, including techniques that will soon allow official translators to reproduce the original document as an image into which the translated text can be inserted.

7. 3 Validity and execution of documents

Official documents must comply with certain requirements to be valid. Those requirements not only vary from one country to another, they also define different stages in the life of a document or set of documents.

From the moment a document is initiated in the source culture until we obtain a valid translation in a foreign country, we can find the following added documents, illustrated on the basis of two certificates of birth (UK and US) and an academic transcript (See Appendix):

Translation process for a birth certificate (United Kingdom)

Source:
1) The source document is an entry in the Registry, which is not physically included in the documentation.
Source text:
2) The first document included in the documentation is the blank birth certificate form. It includes instructions for its completion and in some cultures it may indicate how to correct mistaken information given. As such, this document is not included in the documentation for official translation.
3) The next document is the blank birth certificate form that has been completed and validated by the Registrar of Births and Deaths. This document is legally valid in the source country but not in Spain.
Transition text:
4) The completed form is followed by the birth certificate that is authenticated by the Foreign Office's Hague Apostille. This recognition is usually a blank text that must be completed. In Spain, the official translation will not be valid unless the source document carries the compulsory Hague Apostille.
Translated text:
5) The next document is the translation into Spanish. This document is not legally valid in Spain because it does not meet the requirements for translations.
6) That is followed by the translation into Spanish that has been certified by

the official translator. It will not be valid for certain uses until the official translator's signature and seal have been duly certified.

7) The final document will be the official translation, duly signed and stamped by the official translator, whose signature and stamp have been recognized by the appropriate institution. At present, this institution is the Spanish provincial subdelegation of the Central Government or the Authentications Office of the Ministry of Foreign Affairs. The translation process ends when the document is accepted by the final recipient, such as the Registrar of Births, Deaths and Marriages in Spain.

For the purpose of translation analysis, it could be said that we have obtained a *virtual* document (points 2 and 3) consisting of the fusion between the blank form and the completed form. In this hypothetical document, only the relevant sections that have been completed would remain.

Translation process for a birth certificate (US)

Source text
1) The original document is a blank form (Certificate of Live Birth) that includes instructions on how it should be completed. It is not identical to its British counterpart. The document is validated by the Local Registrar. It is included in the documentation for official translation.
2) The next document is a reproduction of the above-mentioned entry that has been photocopied onto a blank form (Certified Copy of Vital Record).
3) That is followed by the same document, completed and validated by the County Recorder.

Transition text
4) Next comes that same document validated by the Clerk of a Court of Records. This document is valid in the United States but not in Spain.
5) The next document is the birth certificate to which the Secretary of State's apostille of authentication has been added. Without this apostille the official translation would not be valid, since the source document would not have met the requirements established by Spain.

Translated text
6) That is followed by the translation of the document into Spanish.
7) Next we have a document that consists of the translation into Spanish that has been certified by the official translator.
8) The final document will be the official translation, duly signed and sealed by the official translator, whose signature and seal have been recognised by the appropriate institution.

In this case, documents 1+2 constitute the virtual document.

Translation process for an academic transcript

Although American academic transcripts vary considerably, the general format is similar to the one offered here.

Source text
1) The first document is a blank form. If it consists of more than one page, it includes internal elements of control such as pages or letter-headings with data. It also includes information and instructions on how to complete the form.
2) The second document is the form that has been completed and validated by the Registrar.

Transition text
3) The third document is the completed form, now validated by a notary public. The document thus becomes valid in the United States but not in Spain.
4) The fourth document is the former one to which the state's Secretary of State has added an apostille of authentication.

Translated text
5) The next document is the translation of the document into Spanish.
6) The next document is the translation into Spanish that has been certified by the official translator.
7) The final document will be the official translation, duly signed and sealed by the official translator, with the authentication of the signature and seal.

In this case, documents 1+2 constitute the virtual document.

Clearly an official translation does not consist of just one act. The document or documents to be translated are better seen as a sequence of speech acts (Ferrara 1980a, 1980b).

7.3.1 Signature and seal

The execution (or signature, or signature and seal) of a document includes all the steps necessary for the document to be legally acknowledged as valid. It normally includes one or several signatures and the insertion of corresponding seals or stamps. When one signatory validates a former signature and seal and attests its authenticity, we speak of an attestation, authentication, legalization, verification or certification.

When a document is to be used in another country, it must bear annexed the Hague Apostille (if the country is a signatory of the Convention) or an attestation by the Ministry of Foreign Affairs of the target country of the signature of one of its officers in the source country.

When a document consists of several pages, it is the custom to use a complete signature on the last page and an abbreviated one or initials on the other pages. But signatures, like handwriting, differ across countries and cultures. For instance, in Spain there may be two different signatures: the 'full signature', with a usually illegible paraph ("a flourish after a signature, originally to prevent forgery", *Collins English Dictionary*) plus the name, and the single signature, consisting of the paraph only. In the case of a document comprising several pages, all of them but the last bear the paraph of the signature in the left margin and the last page bears the full signature. No indication announces the brief signature, but if you need to indicate it, you can use the word *visé* (French for something like "seen and approved"). In the English-language system there is only one kind of signature, a handwritten name, which is included on the last page while the previous pages bear the 'initials' of the name, at the bottom of the page. *Visé* and initials are thus equivalent. (For a description of seals/stamps and their translation, see section 7.2.3.)

Usually the signatures and seals of official translators are kept in a register (the professional society or association, Ministry of Foreign Affairs, Ministry of Justice or other administrative bodies). The registrars in charge of these registers authenticate the signature and seal of the official translators.

7.3.2 Certifying authorities

Examples of attestations and certifications

Attestation of a copy by a British notary public

I confirm that this is a true copy of the original document produced to me on …..
Signature: ……….., solicitor
[Seal of the solicitor]

I certify this document to be a true copy of the original. Dated this …..th day of …..– [Signed]. – Solicitors.– Address. – ……., Partner)

Attestation of a copy in the US by an officer

True and correct copy. – [Signed]

Certified to be a true copy. – [Signed]

Attestation of a copy by a Pakistani notary public

Correct according to original.

Attestation of a copy in Spain

Attested to correspond with its original. – [Signature]. – [Seal]

Attestation of a copy by a Spanish Embassy/Consulate

Seen at the Consular Section of the Embassy of Spain in ...., and authenticating the signature of .... as, as far as I know, it is genuine.– [Signed]......., Counsellor.– [Seal].– Date.

Attestation by a US notary public

[Signed].– Notary Public.– .... County. My commission expires on.....

Attestation by a notary public in Pakistan

Attested
[Signed]:.........Notary Public Advocate. – Distt. Court Lahore. – Residence. – [Seal]

Attested
[Signed: ....Oath Commissioner. – [Seal]

Attestation of a certificate from a Register in the United Kingdom

Certified to be a true copy of an entry in my custody.
Signed: ...., Registrar
Date:

Attestation of a signature by a notary public in the US

This is to certify that the signatures of the persons on the diploma of........, namely ...., ..., and .... are the genuine signatures of the said persons, who are duly authorized by the laws of the State of .... to sign a diploma.
[Signed]. – Notary Public, ...County. – My Commission expires on ....

Attestation of the signature of a US notary public by a Court of Records

STATE OF OHIO
ss.

County of Montgomery
I, ----------, Clerk of the Common Pleas Court in and for said County, which is a Court of Record, having a seal, do hereby certify that ------------, whose name is subscribed to the certificate or proof of acknowledgement of the annexed instrument and therein written, was at the time of so taking such proof of acknowledgement a NOTARY PUBLIC in and for said County, duly commissioned and qualified and duly authorized to take the same, and to take and certify the proof and acknowledgement of deeds by the laws of this State; and further, that I am acquainted with his handwriting, and verily believe that the signature to the said certificate of proof of acknowledgement is genuine. I further certify that said instrument is executed and acknowledged according to the laws of the State of Ohio. The impression of the

Notary's seal not required to be filed in my office.
In Testimony Whereof, I have hereunto set my hand and affixed the seal of the said court in the City of Dayton, this --th day of--------,
No.   Signed: ------------------, Clerk

Certifying formula of a Spanish sworn translator

This formula is stipulated by law:

Mr/Ms ...., Sworn Interpreter of (language), do hereby certify that the above is a faithful and complete translation into (language) of a document written in (language).
At.........., on ....
Signed:
[Seal including full name of the translator, "sworn interpreter", authorised language, residence and telephone number]

Certifying formula of a Pakistani official translator

Correctly translated from Urdu to English.

True translation of... from Urdu to English.– The translation of this ·Form· from Urdu to English has been examined carefully & found correct. Hence this Certificate to be True.

Certifying formula applicable to an official translation to be used in the United Kingdom

I, ..., sworn translator of English, authorised by the Spanish Ministry of Foreign Affairs, do hereby certify that the following is a true and faithful translation of a .... written in Spanish, presented to me by Mr/Ms ....:

Witness my hand this day of ....
Signed

Attestation of the signature of a Spanish sworn translator

Ministry of Foreign Affairs. – Attestations.- Madrid, on ...... Seen and approved to legalise the afore signature as it is, as far as I know, genuine.. – Signed, Chief Officer, Office of Attestations. [Seal of the Office]

I, ..., General Vice-secretary of the Delegation of the Central Government in Granada, do hereby certify that Ms ...., appears under no. 6 on the Book of Registry of Sworn Interpreters, and she has been appointed by the Ministry of Foreign Affairs, pursuant to Rule 8 of the Decree of this Ministry dated on October 14, 1985 (Spanish Official Gazette 252 of 21/10/85).
[Signed]. – [Sealed]

The Hague Apostille

The Hague Apostille may be monolingual or bilingual, such as the following one, written in English and French:

APOSTILLE
(Hague Convention of 5 October 1961/Convention de La Haye du 5 octobre 1961)
1. Country
   Pays
This public document/Le present acte public
2. has been signed by
   a été signé par
3. acting in the capacity of
   agissant en qualité de
4. bears the seal/stamp of
   est revétu du sceau/timbre de
   Certified/attesté
5. at/à   6. the/le
7. By
   par
8. Number/sous N°
9. Stamp   10. Signature
   Timbre

Signatory Countries of the Hague Convention were, as of March 1999:

Andorra, Antigua & Barbuda, Argentina, Armenia, Australia, Austria, Bahamas, Barbados, Belarus, Belgium, Belize, Bosnia & Herzegovina, Botswana, Brunei, Croatia, Cyprus, Czech Republic, Dominica, El Salvador, Fiji, Finland, France, Germany, Greece, Grenada, Guyana, Hong Kong, Hungary, Ireland, Israel, Italy, Japan, Kiribati, Latvia, Lesotho, Liberia, Liechtenstein, Lithuania, Luxembourg, Former Yugoslav Republic of Macedonia, Malawi, Malta, Marshall Islands, Mauritius, Mexico, Netherlands (incl. Aruba; Netherlands Antilles), Niue, Norway, Panama, Portugal (incl. Macau; Madeira), Russia, Samoa, St. Kitts & Nevis, St. Lucia, St. Vincent & the Grenadines, San Marino, Seychelles, Slovenia, Solomon Islands, South Africa, Spain, Surinam, Swaziland, Switzerland, Tonga, Turkey, Tuvalu, United States (incl. Puerto Rico), United Kingdom (incl. Dependent Territories), Vanuatu, Venezuela, Federal Republic of Yugoslavia (Serbia & Montenegro), Zimbabwe.

7.4 Medium

The medium, as the physical support on which the message is transmitted, can be relevant to official translation, as in any other form of translation.

In official translation there are mainly two types of copies: hard and soft.

(The spoken medium – sight translation and interpreting – lies beyond the scope of this book.)

Hard copies

Hard copies are those that use paper. There are several basic features:

Size: DIN A4 is the most common size of paper used for translation, and indeed for every other kind of written communication. However, in some countries other sizes can be normal. In the United States, for example, some original texts have a larger, 'legal' size, and the normal size is 'American letter'. When transmitted by fax into DIN A4 size, pages become interrupted as part of the text, and a couple of lines can be lost in each interruption. If we cannot check the original, these interruptions should be rendered as *[original interrupted]* or something similar. The fact that part of the text is missing can seriously affect the understanding of other parts that have been successfully transmitted.

Photocopies: If defective, photocopies may interrupt the original. Embossed seals become invisible. Certified photocopies are as valid as originals, and we should mention in our translation that they are certified copies. Although the risk of translating from photocopies is high (see Section 7.2.4), so is the risk of losing or deteriorating valuable originals.

    Photocopies of the translated text are not legally valid. If copies are needed, the client should request them from the translator, who will sign and seal all of them originally and apply a reduced fee to the subsequent originals.

Faxes: Faxes have the same adverse effects as photocopies with respect to legibility, interruptions and manipulation. The problem with legibility can be even worse as faxes transmitted on thermal paper become increasingly invisible. An official translation transmitted via fax cannot be legally valid. A new problem with faxes is that they usually contain, at the beginning of the page, information about the transmission (time, date, sender, number of pages). We must assess the need to translate this information. In some cases we can consider it as non-pertinent, but in other cases (for instance, evidence in court) it can be of importance and we should include it in our translation. The numbering of pages in the transmission message may not be identical to the numbering of the pages in the original; be careful. As to accepting faxes instead of the original, the considerations made for photocopies hold valid.

Fiscal paper: Some official translators prefer to write their translations on fiscal paper. This is not a legal norm; we do not know whether in some countries it is an associative norm. The use of this official paper simply endows the translation with the air of a more formal document.

Soft copies: Soft copies are copies on electronic support: diskette, CD, e-mail, etc. They present the same problems as photocopies and faxes as to the possibility of manipulation, even when they do not usually incur problems of legibility or interruption. If scanned originals are transmitted, legibility and completeness are more likely to be problematic. Official translations transmitted on soft copy are not normally considered legally valid, but this might change in the near future with the consolidation of the electronic signature.

Other fields of translation have seen an increase in the use of telework (working from a distant place and communicating with the client through telephone, fax and the internet). This is not the case with official translation, where a close and almost personal contact with the client is necessary. The use of couriers is characteristic of official translation and makes it even more expensive. Courier expenses are usually paid by the client.

Suggested activities

1) Revise the joint-venture contract and the non-circumvention and non-disclosure agreement included in the Appendix. Underline errors, mistakes, inconsistencies, interference from other languages, style, punctuation, use of capital letters, etc. and edit it.
2) One page of a guarantee has been interrupted by the fax transmission. A clause reads:

    > Notice of default shall include a signed affidavit stating the date payment was due under the Loan, the amount [...] accruing each day, the rate at which such interest is computed, and that such amount has not been received by the Obligee.

    Try to fill in the blank between the square brackets.
3) Rewrite the Pakistani death certificate in Appendix as a series of paragraphs. Remember to organize attestations, signatures and seals in a chronological, logical way.
4) Your customer wants you to validate their own translation (cf. activity 3 in chapter 3). How would you do this?
5) Translate your own birth certificate into a foreign language. Make it an official translation that complies with both the requirements of your own country's authorities and the foreign country's authorities.
6) Which kind of original documents cannot be attached to their official translations? If the final receiver insisted, can you think of any solution acceptable for all the parties?

8. On the Translation of Different Documents

8.1 Birth, marriage and death certificates

In Section 7.3 we saw the process of elaboration and validation of both a British and a US birth certificate. I shall now describe some other problems specific to the official translation of this kind of document.

Administrative bodies

In many countries, the Registry of Births and Deaths also includes Marriages and is sometimes called Civil Registry (as in Spain). In the United States these kinds of registries collect statistical data and so their name changes to "Office of Vital Statistics". This change is reflected in the contents of the certificates, which contain medical information about delivery, vaccination and disease prevention and 'anthropological' data about race.

Certificates under *sharia* differ from others in the sense that paternity or filiation depends exclusively on the father's line. This means the names of the men are followed by the name of their father and even grandfathers, and the names of the women are followed by their masculine ancestors, while the name of the mother (in full, in Pakistan, or partially, in Morocco) are absent from the certificate. In the case of Pakistan you can also find information on caste and religious affiliation.

Personal names

Personal names follow different systems in the world and functional equivalence is not always necessary. There are problems in translating personal names composed of one first name and a middle one (as in English) into systems that normally only have one first name (Spanish). There are problems in translating names with one surname (the father's, as in English) to systems with two surnames (father's and mother's, as in Spanish). There are problems in translating from systems with no distinction between first names and surnames (Pakistan) into systems with this distinction (most of them). The acquisition of a married name can also be a difficulty (*née*, m.s., name before marriage). The solving of these problems rests in most of the cases in the hands of the Registrar, but sometimes the translator can help by both deciphering and translating, acting as a cultural bridge.

There are some common tricks to help solve these problems:

First names and surname	→	Names and surname
Roberto Mayoral Asensio	→	Roberto MAYORAL ASENSIO
	→	Roberto Mayoral-Asensio
	→	Mayoral Asensio, Roberto

Names and surname	→	First names and surname
Anthony David Pym	→	Anthony David PYM
	→	Anthony-David Pym
	→	Pym, Anthony David

We have already pointed out the problem of translating Pakistani personal names. Many other systems can be found. Arabic personal names, for instance, consist of three parts: first name, father's name and grandfather's name; the latter is usually the family name, accomplishing the function of Western father's last name. As for names in Chinese and Hungarian, their first word corresponds to what would be the last name in English.

Transliteration and transcription

An additional problem in translating certificates is the occurrence of names written in a different writing system (e.g. Roman, Arabic, Hebrew, Cyrillic or Chinese). These words are rendered into languages written with a different writing system through different conventions that adapt to the spelling and rules of each language. Even for the same language quite often you can find different transliteration and transcription systems:

Moscow (English)
Moskva (transliterated Russian)
Moscou (French)
Moscú (Spanish)
Mosca (Italian)

We can thus alter identities just by adopting different systems of transliteration (it is not unusual to find different versions of the same name even in the one document). We can also find alterations made, not quite involuntarily, by persons other than the translator.

As the first priority in the translation of personal names is identification, I would not recommend adapting spellings between different languages. I would just stick to the original. Nor would I introduce changes in a document with respect to the original just in order to keep coherence between different spellings of the same name. A different case is that of geographical names, which usually have counterparts in each foreign language. Those names should be translated into their official equivalents (and not only when they come from a different writing system):

>   Khartoum (English, French)
>   Jartum (Spanish)
>
>   Genève (French)
>   Geneva (English)
>   Genf (German)
>   Ginebra (Spanish)
>   Ginevra (Italian)
>
>   Aachen (German)
>   Aix-la-Chapelle (French)
>   Aquisgrán (Spanish)

Non-relevant text

My opinion is that we should exclude from our translation all information re-lated to the publication of the form, and well as instructions to complete the form, since that information is without function as soon as the form is com-pleted. We should also omit the 'optional answers' that are not applicable to the completed form (for example, all the little boxes that were not crossed).

   The effect of omitting this information is to make the translation cheaper, clearer, simpler and stylistically better.

Job descriptions

Human professional activities and trades are not always conceptualized in the same way in different cultures, especially with respect to trade qualifications. They can even be characteristic of a culture and can differ. Usually this infor-mation is not crucial in the certificate and we can use cultural approximation as a mode of translation.

Medical information

Medical information in an administrative or legal document always startles the official translator; it usually demands some research work with physicians and/or specialized dictionaries.

Rank

Registrar certificates from the UK usually include an epigraph for the rank of the father, together with his occupation or profession. This refers to rank in the

British Army or in the Anglican Church; it has no counterpart in many other countries.

Identification of acts

In England and Commonwealth countries we sometimes find a particular way of identifying acts:

> 1 & 2 ELIZ. 2 CH. 20
> 43 & 44 Vic., Cap 13
> Muslim Family Ordinance issued in 1961 (8, 1961)

This can be translated as:

> Act number x of those Acts passed under the kingdom of (Queen Victoria/Queen Elizabeth II…), Chapter no…...

> Act number 8 of those passed in the year 1961

8.2 Academic transcripts and diplomas

Academic documentation may vary substantially between different countries and even inside the same country (as in the United States). These differences affect educational systems, authorities, teaching and non-teaching staff and their categories, fields of knowledge, calendar, examinations, degrees and diplomas and grades.

Clients commissioning an official translation seek the validation or recognition of a course completed in a different country. This validation is the exclusive responsibility of the authorities in the target country and no translator should try to usurp it. But the translator is paid by the person who is trying to appear their best before the authorities, and inevitably, the official translation will be suspected of bias. The consequences of this are various:

- a very literal way of translating is expected
- all the possible means of identifying the original data are to be kept
- the translator should avoid using validating ways of translating, and limit themselves to describing facts, leaving their interpretation to the competent authorities
- where understanding and identification are both necessary, the translator should use two-fold or three-fold translation solutions.

In Section 3.3 we saw the process of elaboration and validation of an academic transcript. We shall now point out some specific problems in the translation of these documents.

Degrees

Multiple solutions, which allow for understanding and identification at the same time, can be used:

Original	Translation (backtranslated)
Bachelor of Arts in Psychology	*Bachelor of Arts in Psychology* [degree corresponding to a first four-year university program of study with specialization in Psychology]

Here the phrase *Bachelor of Arts in Psychology* should be written in the original language in the translation. The duration of the course of study is important as, for instance, a B.A. can last for a different number of years in different countries. This kind of information is important for the authorities.

The same applies to grades:

Original	Translation
B+	*B+* [70%]

Where *B+* in the translation should be written in the original language and somewhere in the translation – if possible – there should be the grading system or at least the pass grade for that institution.

Sometimes the pass grade is not included in US academic transcripts. My opinion is that the information is incomplete without it and you should do your best to give it (including through consultation with the client). If you have to trust the information given by the client, you have a further problem.

As for the marks in British degrees, we usually use a very literal mode of translation, almost by cognates, if the local authorities are sufficiently familiar with systems, which is usually the case.

Grades

As a way of illustrating the frequent lack of equivalence between systems, we shall take a look at the grades system in the United States.

In the United States there is no ministry responsible for the whole education system. The leeway for the different institutions is extraordinarily high when compared with most other countries. A particular system for grading is thus to be expected for each particular institution. The following elements are simultaneously possible:

- Nominal: system based on denominations (excellent, superior, very good, satisfactory, average, passing, barely passing, fail).

- Literal; based on letters, A, B, C, D, E, F, to which signs + and – may be added; E is currently almost absent from university transcripts and increasingly disappearing in High Schools. A+ is quite often absent, sometimes neither plus nor minus are used for the whole scale; sometimes they only use both for B, etc.
- Grade point average: numeric grade going from 0 to 4 (different systems are to be found, for instance: A, 4.0; A-, 3.7; B+, 3.3; B, 3.0; B-, 2.7; C+, 2.3, C, 2.0; C-, 1.7; D, 1.0; F, 0.0 or A+, 4.0; A, 3.99; A-, 3.69; B+, 3.5; B, 3.29; B-, 2.9; C+, 2.69; C, 2.49; C-, 1.9; D, 1.69; F, 0.0).
- Percentage: scale from 0% to 100%; different values can be found, for instance: A, 110-94 or 93; B, 93-88 or 85; C, 87-79 or 76; D78-79 or 70; E, 60; F, 69 or 59.
- Units or credits: units of value assigned to each course; they differ in hours required for 1 unit according to particular courses.

Further, a system based on two only possible grades, Pass and Fail, is possible for some courses. An honorary system of grades (with honours) is also possible for grading individual courses.

The pass grade may be different for each educational institution. Even when the most usual ones are 65% for university and 60% for high schools, we can also find other values, such as 70%.

On the other hand, all educational institutions in Spain follow the same rules, grading systems included. Grades present the following elements at university:

- Nominal: based on denominations (*matrícula de honor* = highest grade, with tuition waived for the following year, *sobresaliente* = with distinction, *notable* = very good, *aprobado* = pass, *suspenso* = fail)
- Literal: there is no literal system as such, only in primary school
- Grade point average: non-existent, although a scale is being introduced: *matrícula de honor*: 4; *sobresaliente*: 3; *notable*: 2; *aprobado*: 1; *suspenso*: 0
- Percentage scale: incorporated as a decimal scale, as follows: *matrícula de honor,* 10; *sobresaliente*, 10-9; notable, 8.9-7; *aprobado*, 6.9-5; *suspenso*, under 5
- Units, credits: the system has been introduced recently.

US and Spanish grade systems might be illustrated as in the following table (although this comparison can by no means be generalized to all cases).

Names of institutions

Names of institutions should be considered as proper nouns and transcribed as such:

The University of Michigan   →   The University of Michigan

UNITED STATES				SPAIN	
letter	denomination	GPA	%	decimals	denomination
A+	excellent/superior	4.00	100%	10	sobresaliente/matrícula de honor
A		3.99	99		
			98		
			97		
A-		3.69	96		
			95		
B+	very good	3.50	94		
			93		
B		3.29	92		
			91		
			90		
B-		2.9	89	8.9	Notable
C+	Satisfactory / Average	2.69	88		
			87		
			86		
			85		
C		2.49	84		
			83		
			82		
			81		
			80		
C-		1.9	79		
			78		
			77		
			76		
			75		
D	Passing	1.69	74		
			73		
			72		
			71		
			70		
			69	6.9	Aprobado
			68		
			67		
			66		
	Passing grade		65		
F	Fail	0.00	64		
			63		
			62		
			61		
			60		
			59		
			58		
			57		
			56		
			55		
			54		
			53		
			52		
			51		
			50	5.0	Passing grade
			49	4.9	Fail

This is unless the institution itself has provided different names for different languages, which is a rather rare case. Transliteration avoids cases where a phrase like "Universidad de Michigan" could refer to several different names in the source country (e.g. The University of Michigan, Michigan University).

Sometimes we use two-fold translation systems if transcription will lead to comprehension problems:

Dartmouth College	→	Dartmouth College [Universidad de Dartmouth College / Universidad de Dartmouth]
High Rapids High School	→	High Rapids High School [Instituto de Formación Secundaria de High Rapids]

Concepts without correspondence

There may be concepts that have no equivalent in other systems. For example:

rank in the class	This does not exist in Spain; some kind of exegetic translation is needed.
grade for a particular course	not used in the United Kingdom
grade for a course of study	used in the United Kingdom but not used in Spain

Deceptive cognates

False friends abound in the translation of academic documents. Here are some between English and Spanish

- *College* in the English-language system is an institution of secondary or higher education; in Spain, a *Colegio* is an institution for primary education.
- *Graduate* in the US corresponds to a second cycle in university; in Spain *graduado* corresponds to a third cycle or to primary education.
- *Secretarios* in Spanish universities are appointed by the academic authorities; a *Secretary* in the English-language system corresponds to an administrative officer.
- *Faculty* in the United Kingdom corresponds to the Spanish *Facultad*; but in American English it also means *teaching staff*.
- *School*, from the American system, translated into Spanish by *escuela*, can be misunderstood as a primary school; *high school*, if translated as *escuela superior* can be misunderstood as an institution of higher education.

- *Bachelor of Arts* cannot be translated as *Bachiller de Artes* in Spain since, in this country, *bachiller* corresponds to secondary education.
- *Class of 1970* cannot be translated in Spain as *Clase de 1970*, as it would not be understood; the Spanish equivalent is *Promoción*.
- *Dean* in the American system corresponds roughly to *Vicerrector* in Spain, whereas a *Decano* is the Director of a Faculty or School.
- *Lecturer* cannot be translated in Spain as *lector*, which denotes a foreign-language assistant.

8.3 Agreements and undertakings

Agreements and other obligations (guarantees, powers, etc.) are among the most difficult documents to translate (and to read). This is due to several factors (cf. Alcaraz and Hughes 2002 for the case of English):

- quite often their authors are not professional writers
- quite often their authors are not native speakers of the language
- there are very traditional style conventions:
  - archaisms
  - use of synonyms and quasi-synonyms
  - references repeating what has already been stated, quite unnecessary most of the time.

These factors affect the first part of our work, comprehension. As to the final part of our work, writing, the temptation to follow the words in the original is strong. This risks making our translation twice as incomprehensible, since the style conventions of the original rarely coincide with those of the target language. Let us have a look at some of these common problems:

Synonymy

1) Doublets and triplets
The following are phrases commonly found in official documents in English:

acts and things	due and punctual
agree and guarantee	duties, obligations and liabilities
agreed and accepted	enter into and execute
aid, assist or permit	execute and deliver
any and all	execution, performance and enforcement
assignees and transferees	expressed or described
author's authorizations, approvals and consents	for and on behalf of
by and between	force and effect

charges, costs and expenses
circumvent, avoid, bypass or obviate
complete and ready
confidential and privileged
consent or permission
construed in accordance with and
    governed by
covenant and agree
covenants and agreements
covenants, agreements
create and constitute
damage, dilute or harm
declared and contained
deduction, abatement
do and perform
document, paper or writing
due and payable
misuse, misoperation
modifications, changes or alterations
name, place and stead
notices and statements
notices, approvals or communications
obligate or bind
over and above
possession or control
power and authority
powers and discretions

powers and provisions
provisions, terms and conditions
ratifying and confirming

forfeited and non refundable
free and clear of and without
give devise and bequeath
given or required
good and valuable
governed and construed

grants, bargains, sells, remises, releases,
conveys and confirms
held and firmly bound
indemnify and hold harmless
individually and separately
instruments and papers
intents and purposes
liens, claims, charges and encumbrances
make, constitute and appoint
might or could
relating to or connected with
release, satisfaction or waiver
revoke, discharge and supersede
set-off or counterclaim
transfer and assign
true and lawful
trusts, powers and provisions
understood and agreed
validity and effects
verbal representations, warranties or
    statements
verification and authentication
well and truly

I would propose simplification as the valid translation procedure here, but most translators, clients, recipients and lawyers prefer to translate into the same number of words.

2) Synonyms and quasi-synonyms

guarantee, guaranty, indemnity,
security, insurance
transaction, operation, venture,
business, trade, deal
submit, present, surrender, give, hand,
deliver, deposit, release, summon
liability, responsibility, obligation, duty
charges, costs, expenses, fees
condition, term, provision, stipulation,
clause

take corrective action, cure, solve
loan, credit
agreement, contract, policy, cover
(insurance)
supplier, seller, exporter
buyer, importer, purchaser
current, valid, attaching, effective, in
force, in effect, outstanding
declare against, claim, implement,
request for execution, demand

I would choose simplification here as well, which in this case means using only one of the variants in the target language.

3) *Different viewpoints in denomination*

principal, borrower, debtor, obligor,
guarantee, guarantor, surety, obligee
lender, creditor, obligee, beneficiary

Here two different procedures are available, either keeping the variation or reducing to only one of the variants.

Lists
books, records, accounts, documentation or other information
company, corporation
court or tribunal
diligence, demand, presentment and notice
import, export or excise taxes, duties, customs and similar charges
laws, ordinances and regulations
law or other rule
notices, applications, demands and requests
provision of law, statute, rule, regulation, order, judgement, decree, franchise or permit
sign, seal and deliver
taxes, imposts, levies, duties or charges
representative, attorney in fact, agent, officer
implement, claim against,
on, upon against, when

My proposal is once again simplification, but not everyone agrees. When there is an equivalent for the different elements and the intention is to mention each of them expressly, there is good reason to translate the same number of words.

Formulas
Most languages have formulas that traditionally separate the different blocks of information in a contract or undertaking. They announce the information that follows, give internal organization to the text, introducing and closing the document, etc. In many cases they are very old and have lost all denotative meaning. To translate their individual words according to their dictionary meaning only produces nonsense; their literal translation is impossible. My proposal is to replace them with functional equivalents in the same type of foreign document:

Original	Translation
....from time to time supplying produces to ...	... , el Vendedor [... , the Supplier,..]
Provided that	Ø
Provided always that	Ø
NOW THEREFORE,	Ø
this agreement witnessed that	Ø
The condition of this obligation is such that	Ø
WE DECLARE: KNOW ALL MEN BY THESE PRESENTS that	Ø
WHEREAS	Ø QUE [THAT]

References

As we have just pointed out, references are often highly redundant. For the sake of efficiency in style, we can sometimes omit them or replace them with grammatically simpler, shorter references, without affecting the meaning:

Original	Translation (backtranslated)
if the Maker fails to make any of the payments on the due dates under any of the ten loan notes issued today by him in favour of the Payee and guaranteed by the Guarantor	if the Maker fails to make any of the payments
at the maturity date agreed upon	at maturity
pay such loss thereunder	pay such loss
notice at its Offices of default thereunder in accordance with provisions of Section 5 hereof	notice at its Offices of default

Implicit information

Other times, contextual meaning makes it unnecessary and redundant to express certain meanings. Concision, understood as a general virtue of style, can benefit from their omission:

Original	Translation (backtranslated)
For good and valuable consideration, the receipt of which is hereby acknowledged, I promise to pay	I promise to pay
...are held and firmly bound unto .... , for which payment well and truly to be made, we bind ourselves..., firmly by these presents...	are bound unto... for which payment to be made, we bind ourselves...
pay such loss thereunder	pay such loss
Seller requires a guarantee as security	Seller requires a guarantee
The due payment of the goods on the due date	The payment of the goods
Shall pay in due course	Shall pay

Repetitions

In the following paragraph we have underlined the terms repeated:

If any <u>action</u> is taken against this Joint Venture, individually or severally, as a result of <u>actions</u> taken or agreements entered into by this Joint

Venture, and any such <u>actions</u> are due to unforeseen circumstances or
circumstances beyond the control of this Joint Venture, each of the Parties shall indemnify against and hold the other Party harmless from any
damages or liability resulting from said <u>actions.</u>

As might be predicted, my proposal here is to omit as many repetitions as possible, for the sake of comprehension and style. Not all languages are as cautious
as English.

Paraphrase

To paraphrase is to put something into others words, restate, rephrase, in order
to clarify the intended meaning. Paraphrasing may thus involve breaking redun-
dancies and repetitions, reducing and simplifying references, and using implicit
information, as we have seen above. More generally, paraphrasing would include cases where these procedures are used in combination.

Let us now see some cases of paraphrase, a number of which may seem
quite radical. The more radical, the less acceptable they risk being in official
translation:

Original	Translation (backtranslated)
For due and valuable consideration, the receipt of which is hereby acknowledged	For value received
Failure by the Principal to make payment when due to the Obligee on the Loan	Failure by the Principal to make payment when due
Programme Returns shall be divided equally with fifty percent (50%) of net earning received by this Joint Venture Partnership from said Programmes and business ventures being paid to JV-1 and fifty per cent (50%) of net earnings from said Programmes and business ventures being paid to JV-2.	Programme Returns shall be divided equally between both parties.
Whereas the Principal has requested of the Guarantor that it obligates itself as Guarantor with respect to the payment of the Loan and the Guarantor is willing to so obligate itself subject to the terms and conditions hereafter set forth,	The Guarantor accepts to obligate itself as such.

The four following clauses mean the same thing:

We irrevocably undertake to pay you on first demand, irrespective of the
validity and effects of the above-mentioned facility and waiving all rights
of objection and defence arising from said facility.

The undersigned therefore agrees to pay on first demand by seller as its
own debt, to seller, against surrender of his written notice stating that the
seller has not fulfilled his obligations to pay the amount of … on its due
date to seller.

Guarantor hereby expressly waives diligence, presentment, demand, protest, notice or acceptance of this Guarantee; notice of any kind whatsoever, and any other rights to which the Guarantor might otherwise be entitled by law. It is well understood that this is a first demand guarantee. As this is a guarantee of payment, not of collection, the obligations of Guarantor hereunder are independent of those of Borrower and Bank shall not be required to take any proceeding or exhaust any remedy, which it may have against the Borrower prior to calling on Guarantor hereunder.

Shall undertake, irrevocably and unconditionally, without regard to the legal validity of the Loan Agreement and exclusively under the condition that the funds have been paid by the Lender to the Principal, to indemnify the Obligee for 100% of the debt due, capital and interest, up to a maximum amount of ... and in addition all costs, interest and damages arising from the default by the Principal to pay at maturity any amount under the abovementioned Loan Agreement.

All four clauses could be transformed into the same simpler one, and translated as such:

Translation (backtranslated): This is a guarantee on first demand.

The following might warrant more extreme paraphrase:

NOTWITHSTANDING the trusts and provisions hereinbefore declared and contained the Trustees may at any time or times during the Trust Period if in their absolute discretion they shall so think fit:
(a) By any deed or deeds revocable during the Trust Period or irrevocable appoint such new or other trusts powers and provisions governed by the law of any part of the world of and concerning the Trust Fund or any part or parts thereof for the benefit of the Beneficiaries or any one or more of exclusive of the other or others at such age or time or respective ages or times and in such shares or proportions and subject to such powers of appointment vested in any person or persons and such provisions for maintenance education or advancement or for accumulation of income during minority or for the purpose of raising a portion or portion or for forfeiture in the event of bankruptcy and otherwise at the discretion of any person or persons and with such discretionary trusts and powers exercisable by such persons and generally in such manner as the Trustees may think fit for the benefit of such Beneficiaries or any one or more of them as aforesaid and for the purpose of giving effect to any such appointment by the same deed revoke any and all or any of the trusts powers and provisions herein contained with respect to the Trust Fund or the part or parts thereof to which such appointment relates and so than in the event of any such appointment the Trustees shall thenceforward hold the Trust Fund or the part or parts thereof to which such appointment relates upon and subject to the trusts powers and provisions so appointed in substitution for any of the trusts powers and provisions

hereof so revoked as aforesaid and in priority to the other trusts powers and provisions herein declared and contained and in any appointment under the foregoing power the Trustees may delegate to any person or persons all or any of the powers and discretions by this Trust or by law vested in the Trustees.

This could be rendered as:

The Trustees may at any time during the Trust Period, at their absolute discretion, appoint new Trustees, revoking older ones and delegating their powers.

Improving grammar and correcting errors

The following are some practical cases of errors found in originals. Sometimes they are just old or traditional expressions. Inadequate punctuation, for example, is often a weak point in the drafting of legal documents. The translators of poorly written texts (written by foreign speakers, non-professional drafters, etc.) must continuously interpret the original in order to restore its 'intended meaning'. They thus translate a virtual, non-existent 'correct' text. Meaning must be restored in order to provide an accurate translation. But anomalous punctuation can also be the result of legal drafting itself: what is strange for the layperson may be the right, most accurate solution for the legal professional. Documents like trust deeds and wills characteristically present a deliberate lack of punctuation in order to suppress unwanted ambiguities.

Errors

The following are fairly typical examples of the kinds of errors that should be corrected when translating official documents, unless there are good reasons not to do so:

Uncorrected	Corrected
Under this Obligees	Under this Obligation
,however, arising.	,however arising.
due on the Loan (provided however, such interest rate shall in no event exceed Eighteen percent (18%), which is in default, such interest to be calculated	due on the Loan (such interest shall in no event exceed Eighteen percent (18%)), which is in default, such interest to be calculated
The Guarantor may, in case of default, to have the right to examine any of the Principal's books, records, accounts, documentation or other information in the possession or control of the Principal relating to or connected with the subject of this Guarantor.	The Guarantor is entitled, in case of default, to examine any of the Principal's documents or information connected with this Guarantee.

Preambles to mercantile texts (agreements and undertakings, paying documents) frequently offer punctuation problems, as they are written in a peculiar way, dividing the first paragraph (sentence) of the document into several different sentences separated by full stops and new paragraphs in an ungrammatical way:

This agreement is entered into this ... day of 1996 by and between:

....

who for the purpose of the joint venture created by this agreement, is acting as "Managing Party", and who shall be hereinafter referred to as "JV-1". The place of business of this Joint Venture shall be at the address of "JV-1" as set forth above.

AND

....

who for the purpose of the joint venture created by this agreement, is acting as "Investing Party", and who shall be hereinafter referred to as "JV-2".

====
THIS AGREEMENT made on ....
BETWEEN:

....

of the first part
-AND-

....

of the second part.
WHEREAS ....
WHEREAS ....
AND WHEREAS ....
NOWTHEREFORE ....

=======
In consideration of your granting a Loan of ..... according to a Loan Agreement signed the ....., 1991 between Yourself and the Company ..... the Borrower,
WE DECLARE:
KNOW ALL MEN BY THESE PRESENTS:
That ...., as Principal and ..... (A Colorado Corporation) authorized to issue this Payment Guarantee while retaining no Liability hereon as a result of being 100% reinsured by its subsidiary ..... which, in turn is 100% reinsured by ....., guarantor(s), are hel and firmly bound unto ....., as Obligee, in the sum of ...., for which payment well and truly to be made, we bind ourselves, our heirs, executors, administrators and successors, jointly and severally, firmly by these presents, subject to the conditions hereinafter following in this Financial Guarantee (Guarantee).

Sixty (60) days after sight Pay to us or our order the sum of £ ... in words ....

At .... sight of this first bill of exchange (second unpaid) pay to the order of
----
the sum of ....
value received

My own choice is to translate the above cases as grammatically correct, well punctuated separate sentences, according to the potential readers' expectations. For example:

At .... sight of this first bill of exchange (second unpaid), pay to the order of -------- ----------------- the sum of .... for value received

Deliberate absence of punctuation marks
Where punctuation has been left out intentionally, the translator should have the option to follow target-language norms:

Uncorrected	Corrected (in British English)
trusts powers and provisions	trusts, powers and provisions
maintenance education or advancement	maintenance, education or advancement
give devise and bequeath	give, devise and bequeath

Standard drafts
As pointed out above, clauses with basically the same meaning are often formulated in different ways. The translator can store their standard drafts and, after minor changes, use the same ones for all cases:

Original	Translation (backtranslated)
Loss shall be reduced by any payments of Principal and/or interest made by or on behalf of Principal before payment by the Guarantor.	Our total liability will be automatically reduced by any payment effected relevant to the debt.
The total amount of this indemnity will be reduced by any payment effected by us in this connection.	
Any partial payment made by us in execution of our obligations under this Guarantee shall be automatically deducted from our total liability.	
The present document will be automatically reduced every time that any payment, relevant to invoices covered by it, is effected.	
neither the text nor the contents	form and content
both form and substance	

Format
Although there are many ways to write agreements, you may find frequently occurring structures that help us to understand, write and translate the document.

A typical macrostructure for an agreement written under common law (Borja 1998) is:

Title: SALES AGREEMENT
Commencement: THIS AGREEMENT, made on (date)
                     BETWEEN .... OF THE FIRST PART
                     AND .... OF THE SECOND PART

Recitals/Preamble:	WHEREAS
	AND WHEREAS
	AND WHEREAS
Operative part:	NOW THEREFORE, THIS AGREEMENT
	WITNESSETH THAT
	NOW, IT IS HEREBY AGREED AS FOLLOWS
	....according to the following terms and conditions:
	ARTICLE 1
	Title
	Clause
	ARTICLE 2
Conclusion:	IN WITNESS WHEREOF, the Parties hereto have
	executed this Agreement as of the date first written above.
Execution:	
Schedules:	

The macrostructure may differ for different countries. A typical Spanish agreement would run:

Title:	(No title)
Commencement:	Place and date [place is not included in the English agreements]
	TOGETHER:
	On the one part ....
	And on the other ....
	[Spanish agreements include parties' particulars such as marital status, National Identity Card or Passport number, address, etc..]
Recitals/Preamble:	INTERVENE:
	[the parties acknowledge each other's legal and corporate capacity to enter the contract and state whom they represent; this information in the English agreement appears somewhere else in the document, i.e. at "representations and warranties"]
	DECLARE
	THAT
	THAT....
	NOW THEREFORE, they deliver this SALES AGREEMENT [title incorporated at his place] according to the following:
Operative Part :	STIPULATIONS
	FIRST. (no title) Clause
	SECOND:
	THIRD:

Conclusion: IN WITNESS WHEREOF, the parties execute this
                                       agreement at the place and on the date first written above.
Execution:
Schedules:

Note that the action of delivering the agreement is expressed in the past tense in
English and in the present tense in Spanish.

Other kinds of obligations, such as undertakings (a letter of guarantee is the
most characteristic case), can have two very different formats in English: a very
long, contract-like one (1500-2000 words) and a short one (about 250 words).
Letters of guarantee in Spanish usually have the short format only. The difference in length for English documents shows how the same substantial meanings
can be expressed in two very different ways and, to a certain extent, justifies
our proposal to simplify expressions as much as possible when translating.

Short denominations

Agreements in all languages give short denominations for the participants, the
instruments and acts. In English they are quite often expressed with capitalized
initials (Disintegrated Biscuits, Inc, the Supplier / called the Supplier / hereinafter called the Supplier / who shall be hereinafter referred to as the Supplier /
the Supplier, etc.). Trends in the use of capitalized initials differ for different
languages. Spanish uses them more rarely than English. We recommend following the English use as it makes the text clearer.

Stress elements

There sometimes appear unusual markers of emphasis in these kinds of texts:

> will <u>NOT</u> accept
> <u>without further</u> authorization
> the Agent <u>MUST</u> follow
> <u>the entire scrow</u> will be refunded

I would not feel obliged to reproduce them; sometimes they are unnecessary, as
they do not add any meaning. When emphasis is really added, it is usually pref-
erable to use lexical rather than typographical means to the same effect.

Here- and *there-* compounds

English feels obliged to specify all the possible interpretations of the legal text,
and does so in quite an excessive way: It uses hundreds of characteristic compound particles that nobody uses in everyday life: hereby, hereon, therein, thereof,
hereinafter, and so on. These particles are mostly unnecessary, since the context strongly reduces the possibilities of interpretation. They also make reading

extraordinarily clumsy and difficult. Using dictionaries to translate them is not advisable as they usually acquire their meaning in the particular context. Not every language follows English in this respect. Spanish certainly does not behave in such a suspicious and overcautious way in this kind of document.

I recommend deciphering these compound particles according to a simple rule that works satisfactorily most of the time: whenever the particle begins with 'here', it refers to the document we are translating; whenever it begins with 'there', it refers to a former document previously mentioned (the Loan Policy if we are translating a guarantee letter; the Letter of Intent if we are translating an agreement; the Insurance Policy if we are translating a certificate of insurance; the claim, the invoice, etc. if we are translating a letter of guarantee, etc.).

'By these presents' means the same as 'hereby', and both of them can usually be omitted in translation as they do not add any new meaning.

Establishing place
After the name of companies, we can find phrases such as

> A Delaware corporation
> A company established in Denmark

These indicate the place where the company was founded. They originate in the United States, where it is important to indicate clearly the state whose laws govern a company's statutes, as opposed to the place where the company carries out its business. This specification is not as meaningful for companies from other countries, but the analogy works.

In translating these phrases, some explicitation is usually necessary. For instance:

> [DELETE]Disintegrated Biscuits, Inc, a society established according to the laws of the state of Delaware, US

Special meanings of some particles, words and phrases
In obligations, *from time to time*, does not usually mean 'occasionally', 'periodically'. It often is an empty formula that does not mean anything (.... *from time to time supplying produces to....*). On other occasions it just means 'at some point in time' (...*or at such other addresses as either party may from time to time designate to the other in writing*)

Similarly, *confirm*, when included in these obligations, does not usually mean "to assert for a second or further time, so as to make more definite" (*Collins English Dictionary*), but just 'state', 'declare', 'certify', 'guarantee'.

The word *understand*, in these documents, may mean 'comprehend' (*the undersigned has read and understood*) but it quite often means 'agree' or 'convene' (*it is understood that both parties...*).

Personalization

In mercantile drafting, English expresses some meaning in terms of names of documents, whereas other languages use the name of the agent related to that document. In such cases, the translation may be said to be 'personalizing' the expression:

Original	Translation (backtranslated)
The Guarantee shall pay to the Obligee	The Guarantor shall pay to the Obligee
A corresponding credit facility is willing to proceed	The Borrower accepts to grant the facility

Formulas valid in the original language only

When something has to be written in a document as a 'citation' in the original language, we cannot translate that into the foreign language, except for comprehension purposes. If our purpose is to instruct our client, it should remain clear that the words are to be written in the original language. For example:

Original	Translation
each draft and documents must state "drawn under Bank"	todos los efectos y documentos deben indicar "drawn under Bank"
will bear on its face the clause "drawn under…"	incluirán en el anverso la cláusula "drawn Under…"
made payable to "……, Attorney-Escrow Account"	se harán pagaderos a nombre de ".….., Attorney-Escrow Account"
writing and executing the following formula on it "For value received, we hereby assign the present Loan Note No 1 and all our rights thereunder to …."	escribiendo y firmando la siguiente fórmula en el mismo "For value received, we hereby assign the present Loan Note No 1 and all our rights thereunder to…"

Literary flair

English obligations can describe companies and persons in terms of appreciative epithets and adverbs that, for other languages, seem exclusive to literary or everyday conversation. For example:

Original	Translation (back-translated)
is willing to are mutually desirous to wishes	accepts
sophisticated investors	investors
a businessman from Marbella, Spain	from Marbella, Spain
the unique services rendered by	the services rendered
experienced	ø
in good standing	ø

My choice would be to omit these value-laden expressions, since they could sound comical or shocking in the target language. In the case of the "business-man from Marbella", for instance, no such profession or occupation would be indicated in Spanish for a contracting individual.

Sections and references
Obligations are usually written with a very strict reference system of Articles, Sections, paragraphs, points, etc. All of these features are introduced by differ-ent systems of numbers or letters or both, along with a rich display of indentations. This structure tries to reflect the logical hierarchy in the document. If our trans-lation is considered as an original document, with no reference to a former source language document, we can vary the references as much as we consider fit. However, if our translation is considered a sequel of an original document, as is the case in official translation, we should respect and reproduce the internal structure and reference system, so that reference to the original elements can be made easily and precisely.

Sometimes original documents have unusual characters for references ("1)."; "1>:"; "1:") or characters that are not acceptable according to the conventions of the target language. For example, English uses lowercase Roman numerals (i, ii., v, x) but Spanish cannot. Since reference and identification are more important than perfect spelling, I would recommend sticking to the original in this respect.

Suggested activities

1) In the joint-venture contract and the non-circumvention and non-disclosure agreement included in the Appendix:
   - underline the phrases and lists containing synonyms
   - underline lists that can be translated by means of an aggregate, global solution
   - underline lists not covered by the above cases and which you can only translate literally.
2) In the same documents, underline the compound particles or words that are redundant either because of other words in the text or because of the context.
3) Translate the clause in the Trust Deed that begins "NOTWITHSTANDING the trusts and provisions…" (in section 8.3) in a literal and complete way.
4) Compare the structure of contracts in English Common Law tradition and your own language following the guidelines that can be inferred from section 8.3.
5) Compare the structure of judicial sentences in two different languages.
6) Translate the US death certificate in the Appendix.

7) Translate the Pakistani death certificate included in the Appendix.
8) Give three different translations of the Letter of Credit in chapter 5 in terms of the following circumstances:
   – your client is the Exporter
   – your client is the Importer
   – your client is a court of justice.

9. Sources of Information

There are two main kinds of information in official documents: legal information and factual or *technical* information, the latter being related to the subject matter of the legal act. You can also find information related to everyday life (as we have seen in chapter 4) or directive information (instructions, etc.).

The ways of accessing technical information are beyond the scope of this work. They differ significantly from the ways to gain legal or commercial information. The official translator usually resorts to specialized companies and to experts (lawyers, accountants, medical practitioners, technicians and engineers, etc.).

Professional translation, as a profitable activity, imposes restrictions on the effort that can be invested in finding information. Researching *ad libitum* may be characteristic of translating as an ideal mental process, as a scholarly activity or as a part of the training stage. In professional activity, however, we simply do not have unlimited time or resources. We have to speed up our research wherever possible. Obviously, the internet is now our most powerful tool, giving quick access to countless sources of information.

In official translation, the following are sources of legal and commercial information:

Text level
- Multilingual texts, including the target language
- Parallel or comparable texts (the same kind of text in the target language, for instance, a bill of lading in relation to another bill of lading), among which the following distinctions can be found:
  - authentic texts vs. texts extracted from form books (collections of blank model documents)
  - texts written originally in the original language vs. translated texts
- Neighbouring texts (close but different types of text, for instance a bill of lading in relation to a charter party), written in the target language.

Lexical level
- Dictionaries, glossaries, specialized terminologies, among which the following distinctions can be found:
  - monolingual vs. multilingual
  - including definitions / without definitions
- Collections of laws
- Manuals, monographs, leaflets, etc.
- Informants.

We will now look at criteria for *assessing* the different sources of information (cf., for a slightly different perspective, Austermühl 2001):

Reliability: Not all sources are equally reliable. Since translators need to limit their research efforts, it is indispensable that they set out a scale or degree of reliability for the information available for each translation. The first sources used should be the most reliable. The first of all sources will be the translator's default source.

Authority is one of the criteria that help evaluate reliability. Information offered by experts and specialized companies is usually the most authoritative. Information from standardization institutions is also highly authoritative, on the condition that the solutions proposed have actually been adopted in the real world.

Accessibility: The translator is obviously restricted to the sources available at the time, place and means of research. The most reliable source loses all value if not available.

Originality: Sources originally written in the target language are the most reliable. A text can be quite authoritative but its usefulness can be significantly reduced if it is a translation of a text originally written in another language.

Specificity is one of the most valuable criteria when assessing reliability. Generally speaking, many people assume that a specialized bilingual dictionary is less reliable than a monolingual dictionary in the same field. From the point of view of translation this is not always true. Very specialized bilingual dictionaries, when high levels of quality are involved, can satisfactorily solve almost all the terminological and phraseological problems in a specialized text. Monolingual dictionaries may be more useful at the comprehension stage. But a good specialized bilingual dictionary, if containing definitions, can be an unbeatable tool for the translator. If a specialized bilingual dictionary deserves our utmost trust, we can even afford to translate some elements of the text without fully understanding them, circumventing meaning (as has been argued above). Many people would strongly disagree with me here, but full comprehension of the text is, in my opinion, more wishful thinking, a desideratum, than a fact of the real, professional world.

Exhaustiveness is strongly linked to specificity. Consulting non-exhaustive sources in a given field wastes the translator's time and renders the translation unprofitable.

Corpora: Dictionaries and glossaries extracted from authentic and dependable corpora are much more useful than sources based on 'laboratory systematizations'. The latter tend to reject borrowings even when they are widely used. The corpora used for this kind of work should be based on authentic texts.

User intended: Dictionaries generally become less efficient when they lose specificity. It is nevertheless common to add general-language entries to the core of a specialized work with the idea of making it the only one necessary.

However, the resulting product is really appropriate only for users who are linguistically less able than the professional translator. This makes the dictionaries more expensive, less useful and full of misleading elements, since it is harder for them to include information about specific sub-fields.

The business of the translator is real communication with real instruments, and not systematization, standardization or exhaustiveness in gathering linguistic data. A translator-oriented dictionary might offer the following characteristics:

- inclusion of paraphrastic and exegetical forms as solutions
- very precise indication of the field concerned
- ranking of different solutions according to their reliability.

Translation solutions have a structural diversity that goes beyond the reach of common lexicographical and terminological entries.

Legal codes or collections of laws are very useful sources of information for legal translation in general, but they are not overly useful for commercial translation, at least for languages that have reliable alternative sources. The terminology in legal codes may differ from that of documents; codes do not usually include the newest concepts; they are not exhaustive from a conceptual point of view. In the case of languages for which specialized dictionaries are scarce, codes can nevertheless be important sources of terminological and phraseological information.

Precedents and case law can be very useful sources of information for legal translation, but their value for the official translator is rather limited.

Collections of official formats or model documents are very useful for the official translator as they constitute a very fruitful source of parallel and neighbouring texts. Such works are more available for some languages (Spanish) than for others (English), especially in the commercial field. However, their usefulness is sometimes rather limited due to their tendency to offer documents written in full rather than with a box layout (a charter party written in full is very different from the document as commonly used in international trade).

The professional official translator is constantly collecting documents in their working languages, anything that may be used one day. They thus build up a personal library covering the basic sources of information. They also build networks of fellow translators and experts for mutual support. Translators' forums on the internet are powerful instruments for this.

In general, professional official translators must constantly try to build and manage the widest linguistic and factual knowledge directly applicable to their work, so that searching for information is reduced to the minimum. They must also combine factual knowledge with operative knowledge, and much of their operative knowledge is directly related to the task of searching for information. The necessary balance is a personal matter.

Suggested activities

1) Make a list of sources giving forms for wills in your language.
2) Use the internet to find translations of three terms that you could not find in the written sources used in activity 1 above.
3) Make a basic glossary of charter parties, using the terms in your country's commercial laws.
4) Compare the above results with those you obtained by consulting the available specialized dictionaries.
5) Compare two different specialized bilingual dictionaries of maritime transportation for your language. Try to find five cases in which both dictionaries offer different solutions. Assess them.
6) Make a list of ten reference sources for the translation of bills of exchange. Arrange them according to the criteria of (a) availability, (b) authority, and (c) reliability.
7) Make a list of the dictionaries and reference works in the field of international trade that you would buy with an equivalent of 500 euros or dollars, assuming you had to build your library from scratch.
8) In the joint-venture contract and the non-circumvention and non-disclosure agreement already mentioned, underline those parts you have not completely understood. Assess, if applicable, whether they can be considered low-risk information – and you would deliver the translation to the client – or whether they are high-risk information – and you should not deliver the translation.

10. Other Professional Aspects

10.1 Fees and estimates

The fees paid to the official translator have traditionally been higher than those for other types of translation, sometimes as much as three and four times the rates for work for publishing companies. However, the way those fees are structured has altered radically in recent years. Here we will look at the classic model, and then at the current reality.

The peculiarities of official translation once meant there was a standard minimum fee per document translated (between 30 and 50 euros in the case of Spain) plus a fee per word or per line of the translated text. Extra charges were added if the translation was into the translator's non-mother tongue, urgent, or involved special difficulties. A further fee was charged for validating translations made by people other than the official translator, and there was still another fee for extra copies of the same translation.

The tradition has been for the professional associations to publish recommended fees for official translation. These fees were even meant to be compulsory in some places, but with time an increasing number of countries have barred professional associations and societies from establishing compulsory fees. All official translators in Spain are obliged to present their list of fees to the local delegation of the central government each January. How are the translators supposed to decide on their fees? The code of ethics for sworn translators in Spain states clearly: "Sworn translators shall not attempt to demand fees lower than those recommended by the Association". So the official recommendations would concern minimums, not maximums.

That said, what really occurs has little to do with what is supposed to happen:

- Almost everyone charges prices *lower* than the recommended fees, which are considered too high by the clients.
- What the translator can charge varies geographically: prices are lower where competition is higher, as in big cities like Madrid and Barcelona.
- Translators propose different prices for different clients, in accordance with:
  - the client's financial capacity (see section 3.4)
  - the workload we expect they will provide us with in the future
  - our personal or professional relationship with them.
- Clients do not accept estimates based on the length of the translated text (even though this is one of the factors that translators take into account), and they demand an estimate before ordering the job (so the length of the translation has to be calculated).

Further, the exceptions and nuances established by the classic model have become meaningless in many cases:

- The distinction between translations into and from the translator's mother tongue has disappeared almost completely.
- Extra charges for urgency are no longer applicable: all assignments are usually urgent.
- The simplicity with which computers make multiple copies makes the corresponding charges too expensive.

Other extra charges have already disappeared, including those for poor legibility or comprehension of the original, or for night work.

On the other hand, the old fees did not include regular activities that should be remunerated, such as appearances in court and notaries' offices to authenticate their translations.

One of the main reasons behind the changes in the fee structure is obviously information technology. In Spain, however, the professional market itself has changed: we no longer have a small number of professionals, nor do our clients have a profile as uniform as they used to. Clients can now choose, and one of the main reasons for their choice will be the cost of the translation. This has had several consequences:

- The regulation of professional practice is currently even weaker than it was in the past, partly giving way to competition and free practice (the problem specifically concerns codes of ethics: it is high time we had a debate on their present force).
- The professional act is no longer uniform, since there is a great variety in both clients and assignments.
- Estimates based on official recommendations can no longer be imposed on the potential client; if they were, we would mostly lose the client.

As a result, I believe that rather than trying to impose fees that do not fit the market, it would be much more reasonable to adjust our services. We should accept that each official translator needs their own estimate system for each assignment and that new ways of pricing might turn out to be more adequate than those of the past. This should include estimates based on the length of the original text, or on the type of text to be translated. Professional associations cannot offer fees knowing that almost no one will or can apply them, and it makes little sense for a government authority to oblige translators to present fees (as in Spain each January) that are largely fictitious.

Many inexperienced translators wonder if their estimates should include the apostilles, authentications, etc. as a part of the main document or as separate documents. The fairest and most reasonable proposal seems to be to consider them all as one single document, as one translation assignment, subject to the one fee.

10.2 Professional associations

As mentioned in chapter 2, there are different types of associations for the defence of translators' interests. They may be specifically for official translators, or for all kinds of translators. In the latter case, they usually include a specific section for official translators. They may also be categorized as either societies or associations.

Professional societies

By 'societies' (*colegios* in Spanish) we mean institutions created by law, in countries where professional practice is also regulated by law. They are the same kind of institutions as those created for lawyers, architects, medical practitioners, nurses or engineers. You are not allowed to practice unless you are a member of this society. The society – and the law – establishes the conditions necessary to become a member; they establish compulsory fees for translation, create ethics committees, validate official translations, ensure high professional standards, help their members with ongoing training, offer some social advantages, and represent their members with respect to the public authorities and society in general.

Although such societies seem to be the institutions most adequate to defend the interests of official translators, they are scarce; few countries have them. The reason is that their creation requires special political circumstances favouring the legal regulation of professional practice. Nowadays, most governments are in favour of deregulating professional practices; they are against the creation of new professional societies for 'new professions'. Even in countries where societies have existed for a long time, governments try to diminish their strength and their regulating power, either by making membership non-mandatory or by reducing the fields in which the society can act legally, such as that of establishing fees.

Professional societies are usually linked to a university degree. This makes their creation conflictive, as some kind of mechanism is needed to incorporate those professionals who are not graduates. Conflict between graduates and non-graduates thus seems unavoidable, at least during a transition period.

Professional societies would seem more viable for those kinds of translation where the translators sign their work, especially for official translation. As a matter of fact, most societies for translators are societies for official translators.

The most prestigious and best-known society for translators is the one in Buenos Aires, Argentina.

Professional associations

Where societies are not found, you are most likely to find an association.

Associations usually correspond to countries where professional practice is not regulated. They are private-law institutions, not public-law institutions, and their regulatory capacity is quite limited. Membership for them is optional; their representational capacity is weaker than that of societies and, usually, they are not allowed to establish prices, organize ethics committees, or validate translations. However, as in the case of societies, associations try to represent the profession, dignify professional practice and offer their members as many services as possible. They are not supposed to contract translations for their members, nor act as a translation company.

It is not unusual for a country to have several professional associations for translators, with different policies or corresponding to different kinds of translators – literary, official, judicial, etc. When different kinds of translators coexist within the one association, conflicts are frequent. These conflicts arise over the importance given to some of them (most typically, literary translators), which is considered unfair by others (most typically, official translators). You can also find professional associations that are specifically for official translators.

Good ideas are frequently spoilt by human differences. All kinds of professional associations find their worst foes within themselves; personal and political differences may ruin associations and may even make them disappear.

The International Federation of Translators is widely accepted as the international association for translators. It has always had a special committee for official translations and edits *Babel* and *Translatio: The FIT Newsletter*.

Below we give a list of professional associations and societies. The list is not exhaustive, as there are many regional associations and new ones are being created while old ones disappear. For further information, visit www.notisnet. org/links/orgs.html (Northwest Translators and Interpreters Society).

Professional societies

Argentina: Colegio de Traductores Públicos de la Ciudad de Buenos Aires (CTPCBA) (www.traductores.org.ar)
Colegio De Traductores Públicos de la Provincia de Córdoba (www.onenet.com.ar/colegio)
Colegio de Traductores Públicos de la Provincia de Santa Fe (042-558627)
Colegio de Traductores Públicos de la Provincia de Catamarca (accacia@ctm.unca.edu.ar)

Uruguay: Colegio de Traductores Públicos del Uruguay (CTPCC) (coltrad@adinet.com.uy)

Venezuela: Colegio Nacional de Traductores e Intérpretes (http://www.conalti.org)

Professional associations for translators in general

Argentina: Asociación Argentina de Traductores e Intérpretes (AATI) (www.aati.org.ar)
Asociación de Traductores e Intérpretes de la Provincia de Buenos Aires (ATIBA) (www.atiba.org.ar)

Australia: Australian Institute of Interpreters and Translators Incorporated (AUSIT) (http://www.ausit.org)

Austria: Der Österreichische Übersetzer- und Dolmetscherverband "Universitas" (http://www.universitas.org/)
Österreichischer Verband der Gerichtsdolmetscher (ÖVGD) (http://www.gerichtsdolmetscher.at)

Basque Country: Association of Translators, Correctors and Interpreters of Basque (EIZIE) (http://www.eizie.org)

Belgium: Chambre belge des traducteurs, interprètes et philologues (CBTIP/BKVTF) (http://www.cbtip-bkvtf.org)

Brazil: Sindicato Nacional dos Tradutores (SINTRA) (http://www.sintra.ong.org)

Bulgaria : Bulgarian Translators' Union (+359 2 65 51 90)

Canada: Canadian Translators and Interpreters Council (CTIC) (htpp://www.synapse.net/~ctic)

Catalonia: Traductors i Interprèts Associats Pro-Collegi (TRIAC) (www.traductors.com)

Chile: Asociación Gremial de Traductores de Santiago (AGTS) (http://www.ceprinet.cl/traductores)

China: Translators' Association of China (+86 10 68 32 66 81)

Cyprus: Cyprus Association of Translators and Interpreters (+357 535 90 51)

Cuba: Asociación Cubana de Traductores e Intérpretes (ctte@ceniai.cu)

Czech Republic: Union des Interprètes et Traducteurs (JTP) (+420 2 241 423 12)

Denmark : Dansk Translatørforbund (http://www.traanslatiors-association.dk)
Dansk Forfatter Forening (+45 31 54 01 15)

Finland: Suomen Kääntääjien ja tulkkien liitto Finlands översättar-och tolkförbund r.y. (htpp://www.megabaud.fi/~sktl)

France : Societé Française des Traducteurs (http://www.sft.fr)

Galicia: Asociación dos Traductores Galegos (xgomez@uvigo.es)

Germany: Bundesverband der Dolmetscher und Übersetzer e.V. (BDÜ) (http://www.bdue.de)
Verband der Übersetzer und Dolmetscher e.V (VÜD) (+49 30 282 93 31)

Greece:	Panhellenic Association of Professional Translators (http://www.psem.gr)
	Panhellenic Association of Translators (+30 31 27 39 77)
	Hellenic Association of Translators-Interpreters in the Public Sector (+30 1 611 72 75)
Guatemala:	Asociación Guatemalteca de Intérpretes y Traductores (AGIT) (http://www.agit-gua.org)
Holland:	Nederlands Genootschap van Talken en Vertal (NGVT) (http://www.ngtv.nl)
Hungary:	Magyar Írók Szövetségének Müforditói Szakosztálya (Bajza utca 19, H-10061 Budapest)
Indonesia:	Himpunan Penterjemah Indonesia (+62 21 489 28 65)
International :	International Federation of Translators (FIT) (htpp://www.fit-ift.org)
Iraq:	Iraqi Translators' Association (+964 1 88 70 577)
Ireland:	Irish Translators' Association (ITA) (http://homepage.tinet.ie/~translation/itacontent.html)
Israel:	Israel Translators' Association (ITA) (http://www.ita.org.il)
Italy:	Associazione Italiana Traduttori e Interpreti (AITI) (http://www.mix.it/aiti)
	Associazione Nazionale Italiana Traduttori e Interpreti (ANITI) (http://www.aniti.it)
Japan:	Japan Society of Translators (JST) (a/s: Orion Press, 1-13 Kanda Jimbocho, Chiyoda-ku, Tokyo 101)
	Japan Association of Translators (JAT) (www.jat.org)
Jordan:	Jordanian Translators' Association (JTA) (+962 2 27 78 00)
Mexico:	Asociación de Traductores Profesionales (ATP) (+525 264 67 87)
	Organización Mexicana de Traductores, A.C. (+52 36 31 01 82)
Namibia:	Namibian Association of Translators and Interpreters (NATI) (c/o Mr. Helmut Nolting, P.O. Box 21289, Windhoek)
New Zealand:	New Zealand Society of Translators and Interpreters (www.geocities.com/Athens/Acropolis/7329)
Nigeria:	Nigerian Association of Translators and Interpreters (NATI) (24 Eric Manuel Street, Surulere, Lagos)
Norway:	Norsk Oversetterforening (www. Boknett.no/no)
	Norwegian Non-Fiction Writers and Translators Association (www.boknett.no/nff)
Panama:	Panamanian Association of Translators and Interpreters (Apartado 1745, Panama 9A)
Poland:	Stowarzyszenie Tlumaczy Polishk (STP) (+48 22 621 56 78)

Portugal:	Associação Portuguesa de Tradutores (http://www.apt.pt)
Puerto Rico:	Asociación Profesional de Traductores e Intérpretes (809-268 41 87)
Russia:	Union of Translators of Russia (+7 095 269 06 46) Soviet po Khoudojestwennomu Perevodou Soyouza Pisateley (7 095 291 94 37)
Slovakia:	Association of Slovak Translators and Interpreters Organizations (APTOS) (+421 7 33 12 94)
South Africa:	South African Translators' Institute (ASTI) (http://www.translators.org.za)
South Korea:	Korean Society of Translators (KST) (+82 2 738 0969)
Sri Lanka:	Translator's Committee of the People's Writers' Front of Sri Lanka (+94 72 77 66)
Sweden:	Sweden Association of Professional Translators (SFÖ) (http://www.sfoe.se)
Switzerland:	Swiss Association of Translators, Terminologists and Interpreters (ASTTI) (http://www.astti.ch)
Syria:	Association des Traducteurs dans l'Union des Écrivains Arabes (+96 3 24 43 29)
Tanzania:	Tanzanian Translators' Association (CHAWATA) (255 49 192)
United Kingdom:	Institute of Translation and Interpreting (http://www.iti.org.uk) The Institute of Linguists (http://www.iol.org.uk) The Translator's Association (authorsoc@writers.org.uk)
USA:	American Translators' Association (ATA) (http://atanet.org) The National Association of Judiciary Interpreters and Translators (NAJIT) (http://www.najit.org) California Court Interpreters Association (CCIA) (http://www.ccia.org)
Yugoslavia :	Savez drua.tava udruzenja knijizevnih prevolidaca Jugoslavije (+381 11 62 60 81)

Professional associations specifically for official translators

Balearic Islands:	Associació d'Intèrprets Jurats de les Illes Balears (34-971 768630)
Basque Country:	Euskal Itzultzaile Zuzentaile eta Interpretarien Elkartea (EIZIE) (34-943-27 71 11)
Brazil:	Associação Profissional dos Tradutores Públicos e Intérpretes Comerciais do Estado de São Paulo (http://www.atpiesp.org.br)
Catalonia:	Associació de Traductors i Intèrprets Jurats de Catalunya (http://www.atijc.com)

Denmark:	Danish Association of State-Authorized Translators and Interpreters (dt@dtfb.dk; www.translators-association.dk)
	Association of Danish Authorized Translators (moos@vip.cypercity.dk) www.translatorforeningen.dk)
France:	Union Nationale des Experts Traducteurs Interprètes près les Cours d'Appel (UNETICA) (www.unetica.fr)
International:	Committee for Court Interpreting and Legal Translation, FIT (Liese Katschinka, http://www.fit-ift.org/english/cti.html)
Morocco:	Corps des Interprètes-Traducteurs Assermentés du Maroc (www.members.lycos.fr/tarajima/index.html)
Norway:	Statsautoriserte Translatørers Forening (STF) (http://www.statsaut-translator.no)
Poland:	Polish Society of Economic, Legal and Court Translators (TEPIS) (http://www.aim.com.pl)
Quebec:	Ordre des traducteurs et interprètes agréés du Quebec (http://www.otiaq.org)
Sweden:	Federation of Authorized Translators in Sweden (FAT) (+46 8 759 03 31)
Valencia:	Associació Valenciana d'Intèrprets Jurats (AVIJ) (Apartado de Correos 9033, 46080-Valencia)

Suggested activities

1) Estimate the number of words of the original joint-venture contract in the Appendix according to the approximate number of words in a line, the approximate number of lines in a page, and the number of pages in the document.
2) Count the number of words in your translated joint-venture contract with the Word Count tool in your word processor. Compare the two results.
3) Make an estimate of the price of the official translation of the joint-venture contract on the basis of the original text, before translating it.
4) Estimate the price for the same contract on the basis of the translated text, either according to the rates established or proposed by your local association or according to your own fees. Compare both estimates.
5) A client wants you to work for them throughout an entire transaction and on various tasks that you cannot foresee (translation from and into your mother tongue, more than two languages involved, official and non-official translation, informative translation, correspondence, telephone, drafting of documents, liaison interpreting, legal and linguistic counselling, etc.). The client wants to know beforehand how much it will cost. How would you estimate the fees?
6) A fellow translator has asked you to do a translation for their own personal

requirements. What fees will you charge them?

7) How much would you charge a penniless immigrant for an official translation?

8) Should official translators always charge the established fees? Can you think of any exception to this?

9) Would you accept to draft a contract in a foreign language? Why?

10) Find out what the taxes and fees are to be paid by a freelance official translator in your country.

11) What are the pros and the cons of professional societies?

References and Further Reading

The following list includes texts referred to in this book as well as a selection of texts for further reading. Since almost all the research and commentary of which we are aware is in Spanish, readers are encouraged to search for further works concerning official translation in their own language or country. In Spanish, important collective volumes are those edited by Pedro San Ginés and Emilio Ortega in 1996 (for French-Spanish) and 1997 (for English-Spanish), both of which include bibliographical articles.

Alcaraz, Enrique (2000) *El inglés jurídico. Textos y documentos*, 4th ed., Barcelona: Ariel.

------ *et al.* (2001) *El inglés jurídico norteamericano*, Barcelona: Ariel.

------ and Brian Hughes (2002a) *El español jurídico*, Barcelona: Ariel.

------ and Brian Hughes (2002b) *Legal Translation Explained*, Manchester: St. Jerome.

Almirati, Gabriela (1993) 'La traducción pública: Marco jurídico y responsabilidad profesional', *Translatio: Nouvelles de la FIT* 1-2: 65-70.

Arnaud, Vicente Guillermo (1958) *Historia y legislación de la profesión de traductor público*, Buenos Aires.

Arrojo, Rosemary (1994) 'Fidelity and the Gendered Translation', *TTR* 7(2): 147-63.

Austermühl, Frank (2001) *Electronic Tools for Translators*, Manchester: St. Jerome.

Austin, John Langshaw (1962) *How to Do Things with Words*, Cambridge, Mass.: Harvard University Press.

Bailey, Catherine J. (1967) *Manual del traductor público*, Buenos Aires.

Borja, Anabel (1998) *Estudio descriptivo de la traducción jurídica: un enfoque discursivo*, Ph.D. Thesis, Universitat Autònoma de Barcelona.

------ (2000) *El texto jurídico inglés y su traducción al español*, Barcelona: Ariel.

Candioti, Ignacio (1993) 'La traducción pública: La existencia de asociaciones profesionales', *Translatio: Nouvelles de la FIT* 1-2: 71-75.

Casas, Francisco Javier (2002) 'La traducción oficial en España'. *Traducción y comunicación* 3: 5-26.

Chesterman, Andrew (1997) *Memes of Translation. The Spread of Ideas in Translation Theory*, Amsterdam & Philadelphia: John Benjamins.

Davis, Kathleen (2001) *Deconstruction and Translation*, Manchester: St Jerome.

El Alami, Dawoud and Doreen Hinchcliffe (1996) *Islamic Marriage and Divorce Laws of the Arab World*, London: Kluwer Law Internacional.

Elena, Pilar (2001) 'La traducción de documentos alemanes'. *Traducción jurada*, Granada: Comares.

Feria, Manuel (1999) 'Inmigración económica y ejercicio profesional de la traducción y la interpretación del árabe en España', in M.H. Larramendi and J.P. Arias (eds) *Traducción, emigración y culturas*, Cuenca: Universidad de Castilla-La Mancha, Grupo de Investigación Traductología, 225-30.

------ (2002a) *La traducción fehaciente del árabe al español. Fundamentos históricos, jurídicos y metodológicos*, Ph.D. Thesis, Universidad de Málaga.

------ (2002b) 'La Mudáwwana. Aproximación al Derecho de Familia marroquí. Lecture given in Toledo, Spain, on July 11 2002 at the Universidad de Castilla-La Mancha.

------ (Forthcoming) 'Traducción jurada, literalidad, ética profesional y unidad de traducción. Un ejemplo práctico'.

------ (ed) (1999) *Traducir para la Justicia*, Granada: Comares.

------, Salvador Peña and Miguel Vega (2002) 'La disposición de Dios o versiones de una frase coránica (111, 154) y lema numismático almohade', *TRANS* 6: 11-45.

Ferrán, Elena (2002) *Las funciones jurilingüísticas en el documento negocial. Un enfoque pragmático*, Predoctoral Thesis. Universitat Autònoma de Barcelona.

Ferrara, Alejandro (1980a) 'An Extended Theory of Speech Acts: Appropriateness Conditions for Subordinate Acts in Sequence', *Journal of Pragmatics* 2: 233-52.

------ (1980b) 'Appropriateness Conditions for Entire Sequences of Speech Acts', *Journal of Pragmatics* 4: 321-40.

Fletcher, George (2000) 'Educational Documents: Translation or Evaluation?', *ATA Chronicle*: 32-6.

Flotow, Luise von (1991) 'Feminist Translation: Contexts, Practices, Theories', *TTR* 4(2): 69-84.

------ (1997) *Translation and Gender. Translating in the 'Era of Feminism'*, Manchester: St. Jerome.

García, Joaquín (1999) 'Informe sobre la traducción e interpretación juradas', in Antonio Bueno and Joaquín García (eds) *La traducción de la teoría a la práctica*. Valladolid: Universidad de Valladolid, 61-80.

Hajjaj, Karima (1999) 'El papel del traductor-intérprete en una ciudad frontera: el caso de Ceuta', in M.H. Larramendi and J.P. Arias (eds) *Traducción, emigración y culturas*, Cuenca: Universidad de Castilla-La Mancha, Grupo de Investigación Traductología, 219-23.

Heltai, Pál (2000) 'Translating Official Texts from English into Hungarian', *Szaknyelv és szakfortdítás. Tanulmányol a Szent István Egyetem Alkalmazott Nyrlvészeti Tanszékénel kutatásaibón 1999-2000*: 34-49.

Mayoral, Roberto (1991) 'La traducción jurada de documentos académicos norteamericanos', *Sendebar* 2: 45-58.

------ (1994) 'Glosario de términos educativos (EE.UU./España) para traductores jurados de documentación académica', *Sendebar* 5: 121-73.

------ (1995) 'La traducción jurada del inglés al español de documentos paquistaníes: un caso de traducción reintercultural', *Sendebar* 6: 115-46.

------ (2000) 'Official (Sworn) Translation and Its Functions', *Babel* 46(4): 300-31.

------ and Ricardo Muñoz (1997) 'Estrategias comunicativas en la traducción intercultural', in Purificación Fernández and José Mª Bravo (eds) *Aproximaciones a los estudios de traducción*, Valladolid: Servicio de Apoyo a la Enseñanza, Universidad de Valladolid, 143-92.

------ and José Luis Sánchez (1994) 'Bibliografía de la traducción jurada (inglés-español)', *Sendebar* 5: 327-38.

Mikkelson, Holly (2000) *Introduction to Court Interpreting*, Manchester: St. Jerome.

Monzó, Esther (2002) *La professió del traductor jurídic i jurat. Descripció sociològica del professional i anàlisi discursiva del transgènere*, Ph.D. Thesis, Universitat Jaume I, Castelló, Spain.

Nord, Christiane (1997) *Translating as a Purposeful Activity. Functionalist Approaches Explained*, Manchester: St. Jerome.

Pavie, Françoise (1982) 'El traductor jurado desde la Antigüedad hasta nuestros días', *Primer Simposio Internacional sobre el Traductor y la Traducción*, Madrid: APETI: 277-91.

Peña, Salvador (1999) 'Valores, además de funciones', *Perspectives: Studies in Translatology* 72: 165-76.

Peñarroja, Josep (1993) 'Los intérpretes jurados', *Sendebar* 4: 263-70.

------ and Celia Filipetto (1992) 'Los intérpretes jurados', in Miguel Edo (ed) *I Congrés Internacional sobre Traducció*, Barcelona: Universitat Autònoma de Barcelona, 501-504.

Puig, Roberto (1990) 'La formación del traductor público en el Uruguay', *Revista del Colegio de Traductores Públicos del Uruguay* 1: 4-9.

Pym, Anthony (1996) 'Multilingual Intertextuality in Translation', in Beatriz Penas Ibáñez (ed) *The Intertextual Dimension of Discourse*, Zaragoza: Universidad de Zaragoza, 207-218.

Robinson, Douglas (1997) *Translation and Empire. Postcolonial Theories Explained*, Manchester: St. Jerome.

San Ginés, Pedro and Emilio Ortega (eds) (1996) *Introducción a la traducción jurídica y jurada (francés-español)*, Granada: Comares.

------ (1997) *Introducción a la traducción jurídica y jurada (inglés-español)*, 2nd ed., Granada: Comares.

Sinland, José (1987) 'El colegio de Traductores Públicos de la Ciudad de Buenos Aires', *Boletín Informativo del Colegio de Traductores Públicos de la Ciudad de Buenos Aires* 10(63): 1-6.

------ (1993) 'La traducción pública', *Translatio: Nouvelles de la FIT* 1-2: 58-64.

Toury, Gideon (1995) *Descriptive Translation Studies and Beyond*, Amsterdam: John Benjamins.

Valero, Carmen and Guzmán Mancho (eds) (2002) *Traducción e interpretación en los servicios públicos. Nuevas necesidades para nuevas realidades*, Alcalá de Henares: Universidad de Alcalá.

Venuti, Lawrence (1995) *The Translator's Invisibility: A History of Translation*, London & New York: Routledge.

Voglino, Mónica (1993) 'La formación del traductor público: Grado y Posgrado', *Translatio: Nouvelles de la FIT* 1-2: 35-40.

Way, Catherine (1997) 'The Translation of Spanish Academic Transcripts: Implications for Recognition', in Karl Simms (ed) *Translating Sensitive Texts: Linguistic Aspects*, Amsterdam: Rodopi: 177-85.

Witthaus, Rodolfo E., *et al.* (2000) *Régimen legal de la traducción y del traductor público*, 2nd ed., Buenos Aires: Abeledo-Perrot.

Addresses

The Internet

RESOURCES FOR TRANSLATORS

There are special sites for reference sources. They offer links to dictionaries and glossaries, bibliographies, organizations and associations, documents and forms, training, lists for translators, conferences and meetings, jobs and other resources. There are many of them, but we are offering just the basic ones to start with. They will lead you to others.

Aljizana	www.ice.uma.es/aljizana
CyberBabel	www.embark.to/cyberbabel
Foreignword.com	www.foreignword.com
Glenn's Guide to Translation Agencies	www.glennsguide.com
Harald Rebling's Home Page	www.ourworld.compuserve.com/
	homepages/H_Rebling
iLoveLanguages	www.ilovelanguages.com
Inter-Tradu	www.inter-tradu.com
Joao Roque Dias' Web Site	www.jrdias.com
Marcia Klingensmith's Home Page	www.pitt.edu/~mrkst19/translation.html
Michael Gierhake's Language and Translation Links	www.geocities.com/Athens/
	Acropolis/3137/index.html
NAJIT	www.najit.org
Neotext	www.geocities.com/SoHo/Workshop/1478
O Traductor Virtual	www.uvigo.es/webs/sli/virtual/titulo.htm
Peter Sandrini's Resources for Translators and Interpreters	
	www.homepage.uibk.ac.at/~c61302
The Language Hub	www.cetrodftt.com/translate.htm
The Translation Factory	www.ahost4u.com/zak/pageprin.htm
The Translator's Home Companion	www.lai.com
Trados Links for Translators	www.trados.com/english/links/intlink9/htm
Translate	www.translate.com.br
Translation Journal	www.accurapid.com
Web del Traductor Jurídico	www.gitrad.uji.es/index_es.html
Xlation.com	www.xlation.com

LISTS FOR TRANSLATORS

Below are communities of translators created in order to exchange information, promote contacts, solve translation problems, debate common issues, etc., all at the highest speed. This is the most efficient way to collaborate with colleagues.

Court Interpreters	majordomo@colossus.net
E-listas	www.elistas.net/lista/tradjur/archivo
Forensic Linguistics	mailbase@mailbase.ac.uk
GlossPost	www.groups.yahoo.com/group/GlossPost
Lantra-L	www.geocities.com/Athens/7110/lantra.htm
Legal Translators	groups.yahoo.com/group/legaltranslators
NAJIT Mail Lists	www.egroups.com/list/courtinterp-l
Proz.com	www.proz.com
Traducción	www.rediris.es/list/info/traduccion.es.html
Translist	www.groups.yahoo.com/group/translist
UACINOS	www.groups.yahoo.com/group/uacinos
	www.egroups.com/list/courtinterp-spanish

DOCUMENTS AND FORMS

Some sites offer collections of documents and forms that can be used as parallel or neighbouring texts:

Everyform	www.everyform.net
FindForm	www.findform.com
Juris International	www.jurisint.org/pub/02/en/index.htm
	www.legaldocs.com
	www.search.yahoo.com/bin/search?p=legal+forms

Journals and newsletters

ATA Chronicle
Publisher: ATA, (www.atanet.org), USA
Babel: International Journal of Translation
Editor: FIT (www.fit-ift.org; www.benjamins.com)
Boletín de APETI
Publisher: Asociación Profesional Española de Traductores e Intérpretes (APETI), Madrid, Spain
No longer published
Butlletí de l'Associació de Traductors i Intèrprets Jurats de Catalunya
Editor: Josep Peñarroja Fa (jppf@eresmas.net), Associació de Traductor i Intèrprets Jurat de Catalonia, Spain
El Lenguaraz
Published by: Colegio de Traductores Públicos de la Ciudad de Buenos Aires (www.traductores.org.ar), Argentina

Proteus

Published by: NAJIT, USA (proteus@najit.org)

Revista del Colegio de Traductores Públicos de Uruguay

Published by: Colegio de Traductores Públicos de Uruguay, Montevideo, Uruguay

Translatio: Nouvelles de la FIT

Published by: FIT (www.fit-ift.org; www.benjamins.com)

TRIAC informa: Boletín de Traductors i Intèrprets Associats pro-Col.legi

Published by: TRIAC (Traductors i Intèrprets Associats pro-Col.legi), (guidini@jazzfree.com) Catalonia, Spain

Voces

Published by: Colegio de Traductores Públicos de la Ciudad de Buenos Aires (www.traductores.org.ar), Argentina

Appendix

[Letterhead: "BANK OF ENGLAND (BE) METAL"][Letterhead: "Sagisag ng Pangulo ng Pilipinas"]

[Stamp: "RECEIVED, BANK OF ENGLAND"]

No. ....
Date ....

Subject
   ISSUE OF LONG TERMS OF VARIOUS DENOMINATIONS AND IN VARI-
OUS CURRENCIES BY THE PHILIPPINE GOVERNMENT TO SECURE SUMS
PRODUCING IN THE AGGREGATE AND OF THE EFFECTIVE SUM OF THE
EQUIVALENT OF .... METRIC TONS OF GOLD DEPOSIT PLUS THE EX-
PENSES OF ISSUE OF NEGOTIATION AND OF DELIVERY.

GENERAL AGREEMENT
NATURE:
   These presents entered into between the Government of England here in after the
Philippine Government of the one part and President ...., as the holder of ... metric
tons. Gold Metal 99.999 being issued under the provision of the prints, referred to
as the holder of the other part witnesseth as follows.

1. The present the Gold Metal 99.999 ..... Metric Tons issued here under
   bind validly of the President of the Republic of the Philippine ....., there
   of for the time being.
2. In virtue of all the power means are into enabling the England government to have determined to contract in a manner appearing as a loan which
   shall be called and known as ..... and referred to as the Expert's Plan.
   Embodied in the report dated the .... day of ....of the First Committee
   of experts, appointed by the Reparation Commission constituted under
   the Treaty of Versailles, is the means of balancing the budget an the
   measure is taken to stabilize the currency of Philippine Government.
3. Any portion of the loan of the English government, shall give to the holder
   an acknowledgement in writing, under the hand of the Minister of Finance for the time being that the England government is indebted to the
   holder to an amount equivalent and in the same currency as a portion of

the loan about to be issued, carrying interest at the rate to be specified in the denomination of such issued; payable by half years installments; and the England Government hereby covenants with that as when the principal Bank Statement secured by the Deposit Code Guarantee to be issued by the Bank of England government and will pay in respective currencies of issue holder or those whose denomination ought to be redeemed or paid accordance with the provisions of the present and the provisions of the relative denomination. The holder interest on the principal money secured by their denomination and shall also pay all charges of commissions and other payments to be made and payable in half yearly installments. In every year at such place or places and such matter as the holder shall direct and the England government hereby further covenants that nothing contained in the Expert's Plan or in any agreement; Protocol Act of Parliament or bringing into operation such plan excluding only these presents and the finance of central Ministry issued under such limit, restrict or vary or be deemed to limit, restrict or vary the obligation of the England government, under the preceding covenant or any other covenant or enlargement contained in these presents or any Certificate issued here under.

4. The whole deposit shall be redeemed not later than the Certificates not yet surrendered for replacement shall remain legal matures on ... Provisions for the redemption of the said deposit issued and payable in England government dollars, shall be made by means of equal twenty-five annual payment; each such payment is to be sufficient to redeem each such issues as part of the contained of the benefits, here of, the principal interest and other money specified to become in all present and future generation of the Philippine government.

5. In case any of said International Certificate at any time become mutilated, No . .... the based on the decision international certificate of obligations or like tinor and date will be issued by the England government in exchange for an upon cancellation of the deposit code guarantee mutilated and its documents or in lieu of the denomination, so destroyed or lost and its documents. But in a case of destroyed or lost deposit code only upon receipt by the holder and a representative of the England Government of evidence, and is satisfactory to them, the that guarantee and documents were destroyed or lost and upon receipt also as a satisfactory indebtnity.

6. These presents shall be printed in English language and all definite certificate to be issued by the England government in respect of the said holder and documents shall be printed in English and England languages and where requires the language of the country in which such respective shall be issued. A copy of the presents in the English language shall endorse on all definite legalized transaction in the event of any divergence between the text, then the text shall prevail.

7. No incurve obligation on the part of the England government shall be

deemed to have been created by the reason only fact that besides the acknowledgements of the indebtedness of the England government, here in contained or provided for acknowledgements of indebtedness, shall also be contained and definitely issued in accordance with these presents. Being duly empowered to bind as well, England government and PHIL-IPPINE government as any government there of for the time being, we undersigned being the present president of the Philippine and England government with the Minister for the finance, have set our hearts and seal this … day of …..

[Illegible signature]   [Illegible signature]

……

President   Corporate Secretary of the
Republic of the Philippines   International Insurance Company

[Raised Seal: "the President of Philippines"]   [Illegible signature]
                                                   Chairman of the
                                                   International Insurance Company

DQ 311776

[Printed by authority of the Registra...]

B. Cert.
R.B.D.

CERTIFIED COPY of an **ENTRY OF BIRTH**
Pursuant to the Births and Deaths Registration Act 1953

The statutory fee for this certificate is 3s. 9d.
Where a search is necessary to find the entry,
a search fee is payable in addition.

Registration District HARINGEY

1968. Birth in the Sub-district of HORNSEY in the LONDON BOROUGH OF HARINGEY

No.	1 When and where born	2 Name, if any	3 Sex	4 Name, and surname of father	5 Name, surname, and maiden surname of mother	6 Occupation of father	7 Signature, description, and residence of informant	8 When registered	9 Signature of registrar	10* Name entered after registration
248	Eighth June 1968 11 Alexandra Park Road		Girl		formerly of 23 Avenue Hornsey	Cafe Proprietor	K. Demetriou Mother 23 Rathcoole Avenue N.8.	Twelfth June 1968	Gladys E. Hider Registrar.	

I, GLADYS ELEANOR HIDER , Registrar of Births and Deaths for the Sub-district of HORNSEY , in the LONDON BOROUGH OF HARINGEY
do hereby certify that this is a true copy of the entry No. 248 in the Register of Births for the said Sub-district, and that such Register is now legally in my custody.

WITNESS MY HAND this 13th day of June , 19 68 .

*See note overleaf.

CAUTION.—Any person who (1) falsifies any of the particulars on this certificate, or (2) uses a falsified certificate as true, knowing it to be false, is liable to prosecution.

Registrar of Births and Deaths

INSERTION OF NAME IN COLUMN 10 OF BIRTH REGISTER

(1)   A christian name given to a child in baptism or a forename given otherwise than in christian baptism before the expiration of twelve months from the date of registration of its birth may be inserted in Column 10 of the entry in the birth register under the procedure provided by Section 13 of the Births and Deaths Registration Act 1953. If the parents or guardians wish to avail themselves of this facility at any time, they must deliver a certificate of christian baptism or if the child has not been baptised, a certificate of naming to the superintendent registrar having custody of the register in which the birth was registered. Either certificate must be in the prescribed form and can be obtained on application to any registrar.

(2)   The christian name or the forename given not in baptism, given after registration and entered in Column 10 supersedes that given in Column 2.

(3)   Were, however, a child was given a name in baptism and this name is entered in Column 2, the christian name cannot be altered by the substitution of a forename in column 10 given otherwise than in baptism.

This certificate is issued in pursuance of the Births and Deaths Registration Act 1953. Section 34 provides that any certified copy of an entry purporting to be sealed or stamped with the seal of the General Register Office shall be received as evidence of the birth or death to which it relates without any further or other proof of the entry, and no certified copy purporting to have been given in the said Office shall be of any force or effect unless it is sealed or stamped as aforesaid.

CERTIFICATION OF VITAL RECORD

COUNTY of SANTA CLARA
SAN JOSE, CALIFORNIA

CERTIFICATE OF LIVE BIRTH

STATE OF CALIFORNIA—DEPARTMENT OF PUBLIC HEALTH

THIS CHILD	1. NAME OF CHILD—FIRST NAME	1b. MIDDLE NAME	1c. LAST NAME
	2. SEX Male	3a. THIS BIRTH, SINGLE, TWIN Single	4. DATE OF BIRTH October 23, 1970	4b. HOUR 2:31 P
PLACE OF BIRTH	5a. PLACE OF BIRTH—NAME OF HOSPITAL Kaiser Permanente Medical Center		5b. STREET ADDRESS Blvd	5c. INSIDE CITY CORPORATE Yes
	5d. CITY OR TOWN Santa Clara		5e. COUNTY Santa Clara	
MOTHER OF CHILD	6a. MAIDEN NAME OF MOTHER—FIRST NAME	6b. MIDDLE NAME	6c. LAST NAME (MAIDEN SURNAME)	7. BIRTHPLACE Illinois
	8. AGE OF MOTHER 33	9. COLOR OR RACE OF MOTHER Caucasian	10a. RESIDENCE OF MOTHER	10b. INSIDE CITY CORPORATE Yes
	10c. RESIDENCE OF MOTHER—CITY OR TOWN Santa Clara		10d. RESIDENCE OF MOTHER—COUNTY Santa Clara	10e. RESIDENCE OF MOTHER—STATE California 95051
FATHER OF CHILD	11a. NAME OF FATHER—FIRST NAME	11b. MIDDLE NAME	11c. LAST NAME	12. BIRTHPLACE Illinois
	13. AGE OF FATHER 34	14. COLOR OR RACE OF FATHER Caucasian	15a. PRESENT OR LAST OCCUPATION Physician	15b. KIND OF INDUSTRY OR BUSINESS Medical
INFORMANT'S CERTIFICATION	I HEREBY CERTIFY THAT I HAVE REVIEWED THE ABOVE STATED INFORMATION AND THAT IT IS TRUE AND CORRECT TO THE BEST OF MY KNOWLEDGE	16a. PARENT OR OTHER INFORMANT—SIGNATURE		16b. DATE Oct. 26, 1970
ATTENDANT'S CERTIFICATION	I HEREBY CERTIFY THAT I ATTENDED THIS BIRTH AND THAT THE CHILD WAS BORN ALIVE AT THE HOUR, DATE AND PLACE STATED ABOVE	17a. PHYSICIAN SIGNATURE		17b. DATE October 23, 1970
		17c. Donald L. Bebehsee, M.D. 900 Kiely Blvd. Santa Clara		C-24890
LOCAL REGISTRAR	18.	19. LOCAL REGISTRAR—SIGNATURE		20. NOV 12 1970

BELOT, WISCONSIN
PERMANENT RECORD

Degree Conferred _____ Major(s) _____ Honors _____ Dept. Honors _____ G.P.A. _____

ADMITTED FROM: Jardines de Caparra High School
Bayamón, Puerto Rico

BIRTHDATE Dec. 3, 1961 Sex M

DEPT	COURSE	TITLE OF COURSE	UNITS	GRADE	POINTS
FALL 1979		**TERM AVG 2.150**			
ART	120	INTRO TO ART HISTORY	1.000	D	1.000
SPAN	250	INTRO TO SPAN LITERATURES	1.000	B	3.000
HIST	100	HIST OF WEST CIV-1200-1648	1.000	C+	2.300
FRENCH	110	INTERMEDIATE FRENCH I	1.000	C+	2.300
UP 4.000		GRP 8.600			
		CUM AVG 2.150	4.000		8.600
SPRING 1980		**TERM AVG 2.075**			
CHEM	100	FUNDAMENTAL CHEMISTRY I	1.000	D	1.000
POR-SC	100	ACADEMIC WRITING	1.000	C+	2.300
ENG	105	20TH CENTURY AM LITERATURE	1.000	C	2.000
SPAN	260	INTRO TO SP. AM. LIT	1.000	B	3.000
UP 8.000		GRP 16.900			
		CUM AVG 2.112	4.000		8.300
FALL 1980		**TERM AVG .371**			
ECON	101	PRINCIPLES MACROECONOMICS	1.000	F	
GOV	110	AM NAT GOV AND POLITICS	1.000	D+	1.300
FRENCH	230	FREN CONVERSATION-COMP I	1.000	F	
C.S.	101	INTRO-COMPUTER PROGRAMMING	.500	F	
UP 9.000		GRP 18.200			
		CUM AVG 1.583	1.000		1.300
SPRING 1981		**TERM AVG 2.775**			
ENG	190	LITERARY STUDY	1.000	C-	1.700
SPAN	370	GOLDEN AGE LITERATURE	1.000	A-	3.700
SPAN	380	STUDIES IN HISPANIC LIT	1.000	A-	3.700
FRENCH	235	FREN CONVERSATION-COMP II	1.000	C	2.000
UP 13.000		GRP 29.300			
		CUM AVG 1.890	4.000		11.100

DEPT	COURSE	TITLE OF COURSE	UNITS	GRADE	POINTS
FALL 1981					
Anth	105	Archaeology & Prehistory			
Hist	385	Topics in Hist/World War II			
Hist	222	Roman Civilization			
Span	395	TA Spanish			
		Changed to VACATION October 21, 1981			
SPRING 1982		VACATION TERM			
FALL 1982		**TERM AVG 1.233**			
POR-SC	227	LAT AM. REVOL&CULTURE	1.000	A	4.00
ANTHRO	100	SOCIETY AND CULTURE	1.000	C	2.00
SPAN	395	TA (Span 100)	.500	CR	
SPAN	394	SP PROB: Atrapados en la telaraña transitoria de los años '30	1.000	†A	3.70(
UP 16.000		GRP 39.000			
+ .500		CUM AVG 2.108	3.500		9.70(
SPRING 1983		**TERM AVG 3.767**			
SPAN	380	STUDIES IN HISPANIC LIT	1.000	A	4.00(
COMPLT	230	COL NEG BL LIT OF PROTEST	1.000	B+	3.30(
ANTHRO	330	CONTEMP CULT LATIN AMER	1.000	A	4.00(
UP 19.000		GRP 50.300			
+ .500		CUM AVG 2.340	3.000		1.30(
FALL 1983		**TERM AVG 3.286**			
ID-STD	230	FILM ART & SOCIETY	1.000	B+	3.30(
SPAN	394	SP PROB:Advanced Spanish Comp	1.000	B	3.00(
SPAN	394	SP PROB*	1.000	A-	3.70(
MUSIC	100	INTRO TO MUSIC	.500	B	1.50(
		*El espejo como modelo estructural del relato en los cuentos de Borges			
UP 22.500		GRP 61.800			
+ .500		CUM AVG 2.472	3.500		11.500

Beloit College
BELOIT, WISCONSIN
PERMANENT RECORD

BIRTHDATE Dec. 3, 1961
Sex M

STUDENT

ADMITTED FROM: Jardines de Caparra High School
Bayamon, Puerto Rico

DEPT.	COURSE	TITLE OF COURSE	HOURS	GRADE	POINTS
SPRING 1984		TERM AVG 2.800			
CLASS	100	LENIN & GREEK PHIL	1.000	B	3.000
CLASS	225	MYTH & MONUMENTS	1.000	D+	1.300
ANTHRO	325	HIGH CIV OF ANTIQUITY	1.000	A	4.000
IO-STD	233	EPIC, ART & FILM	1.000	C	2.000
SPAN	380	STUDIES IN HISPANIC LIT	1.000	A-	3.700
UP 27.500		GRP 75.800	5.000		14.000
+ .500		CUM AVG 2.527			
Fall	1984	VACATION TERM			
SPRING	1985	VACATION TERM			

IN ACCORDANCE WITH THE FAMILY EDUCATIONAL
RIGHTS AND PRIVACY ACT OF 1974, THIS INFORMA-
TION IS PROVIDED FOR YOU ON THE CONDITION
THAT YOU WILL NOT PERMIT ANY OTHER PARTY
TO HAVE ACCESS TO THIS INFORMATION WITH-
OUT THE WRITTEN CONSENT OF THE STUDENT

Edward F. Mayer
REGISTRAR

Muncipal Corporation Rawalpindi   823

Copy of Death Certificate from Muncipal Corporation Rawalpindi

Regd No:	Date & year when death	Name of deceased	Name of deceased marriage with his husband name	Sex	Age	Profession Caste Religion of deceased	Name of Mohallah	House No. Sector	Cause of death	period of deceased	Name of informer	Date Month year death regd.	Name of Doctor with address	Name Remark
1185	15-7-1991 Fifteen July Nineteen hundred ninety one		wife of	Female	About 20 years	House hold Kashmiri-Islam	Rawalpindi Sector, House No.		Accident	3 days (three days)		25-7-1991	District Head Quarter Hospital, Rawalpindi	I.Ilaqa Counsillor Ch:Riaz

CERTIFIED TRUE COPY

Sd/xx
Chief Medical Officer
of Health Muncipal
Corporation Rawalpindi.

Sd/xx
Superintendent Health
Muncipal Corporation
Rawalpindi.

Sd/xx
Birth & Death
Clerk
Muncipal Corporation
Rawalpindi.

ATTESTED
(ABDUL MAJID AKRAM)
Sector Forth
Islamabad.
O.2.4.1993

STATE OF FLORIDA

OFFICE of VITAL STATISTICS

CERTIFIED COPY

CERTIFICATE OF DEATH
FLORIDA

LOCAL FILE NO. *121*

1. DECEDENT'S NAME (First, Middle, Last)	
2. SEX	Female
3. DATE OF DEATH (Month, Day, Year)	February 27, 1990
4. SOCIAL SECURITY NUMBER	
5a. AGE-Last Birthday (years)	84
5b. UNDER 1 YEAR (Months / Days)	
5c. UNDER 1 Day (Hours / Minutes)	
6. DATE OF BIRTH (Month, Day, Year)	September 27, 1905
7. BIRTHPLACE (City and State or Foreign Country)	Granada Spain
8. WAS DECEDENT EVER IN U.S. ARMED FORCES? (Yes or No)	No

9a. PLACE OF DEATH (Check only one; see instructions on other side)

HOSPITAL: ☐ Inpatient ☐ ER/Outpatient ☐ DOA OTHER: ☐ Nursing Home ☐ Residence ☐ Other (Specify)

9b. INSIDE CITY LIMITS? (Yes or No) — Yes

9c. FACILITY NAME (If not institution, give street and number)	9d. CITY, TOWN, OR LOCATION OF DEATH	9e. COUNTY OF DEATH
Depoo Hospital	Key West	Monroe

10a. DECEDENT'S USUAL OCCUPATION	10b. KIND OF BUSINESS/INDUSTRY	11. MARITAL STATUS — Married, Never Married, Widowed, Divorced (Specify)	12. SURVIVING SPOUSE (If wife, give maiden name)
Housewife	House Work	Married	

13a. RESIDENCE — STATE	13b. COUNTY	13c. CITY, TOWN, OR LOCATION	13d. STREET AND NUMBER
Florida	Monroe	Key West	

13e. INSIDE CITY LIMITS? (Yes or No)	13f. ZIP CODE	14. WAS DECEDENT OF HISPANIC OR HAITIAN ORIGIN? (Specify No or Yes — If yes, specify Haitian, Cuban, Mexican, Puerto Rican, etc.)	15. RACE — American Indian, Black, White, etc. Specify:	16. DECEDENT'S EDUCATION (Specify only highest grade completed) Elementary/Secondary (0-12) / College (1-4 or 5+)
Yes	33040	☒ No ☐ Yes Specify:	White	12

17. FATHER'S NAME (First, Middle, Last)	18. MOTHER'S NAME (First, Middle, Maiden Surname)

19a. INFORMANT'S NAME (Type/Print)	19b. MAILING ADDRESS (Street and Number or Rural Route Number, City or Town, State, Zip Code)
	1213 20th St. Key WEst Fl. 33040

20a. METHOD OF DISPOSITION	20b. PLACE OF DISPOSITION (Name of cemetery, crematory, or other place)	20c. LOCATION — City or Town, State
☒ Burial ☐ Cremation ☐ Removal from State ☐ Donation ☐ Other (Specify)	Key WEst City Cemetery	Key WEst Florida

21a. SIGNATURE OF FUNERAL SERVICE LICENSEE OR PERSON ACTING AS SUCH	21b. LICENSE NUMBER (of Licensee)	21c. NAME AND ADDRESS OF FACILITY
Jeffrey Dean	2550	Dean-Lopez Funeral Home 418 Simonton Street Key WEst Fl. 33040

22a. To the best of my knowledge, death occurred at the time, date and place and due to the cause(s) as stated.

(Signature and Title) *Peter J Canova*

22b. DATE SIGNED (Mo., Day, Yr.)	22c. HOUR OF DEATH
2/28/90	4:47 am

22d. NAME OF ATTENDING PHYSICIAN IF OTHER THAN CERTIFIER (Type or Print)

23a. On the basis of examination and/or investigation, in my opinion death occurred at the time, date and place and due to the cause(s) and manner as stated.

(Signature and Title)

23b. DATE SIGNED (Mo., Day, Yr.)	23c. HOUR OF DEATH	23d. PRONOUNCED DEAD (Mo., Yr.)	23e. PRONOUNCED DEAD (Hour)
	M		M

24. NAME AND ADDRESS OF CERTIFIER (PHYSICIAN, MEDICAL EXAMINER) (Type or Print)	25c. DATE REGISTERED
Dr. Robert Caraway M.D. 3428 N. Roosevelt Boulevard Key WEst Fl. 33040	March 5, 1990

25a. SUBREGISTRAR — SIGNATURE AND DATE	25b. LOCAL REGISTRAR — SIGNATURE
	Lois Gallagher

26. PART I. Enter the diseases, injuries, or complications that caused the death. Do not enter the mode of dying such as cardiac or respiratory arrest, shock, or heart failure. List only one cause on each line.

	Cause	Approximate Interval Between Onset and Death
IMMEDIATE CAUSE (Final disease or condition resulting in death)	a. Extensive left lung pneumonia	2 days
DUE TO (OR AS A CONSEQUENCE OF):		
Sequentially list conditions, if any, leading to immediate cause. Enter UNDERLYING CAUSE (Disease or injury that initiated events resulting in death) LAST.	b. possible mucus plug	
DUE TO (OR AS A CONSEQUENCE OF):		
	c.	
DUE TO (OR AS A CONSEQUENCE OF):		
	d.	

PART II. Other significant conditions contributing to death but not resulting in the underlying cause given in Part I.	27a. WAS AN AUTOPSY PERFORMED? (Yes or No)	27b. WERE AUTOPSY FINDINGS AVAILABLE PRIOR TO COMPLETION OF CAUSE OF DEATH? (Yes or No)	28. CASE REPORTED TO MEDICAL EXAMINER? (Yes or No)
Acute renal insufficiency	No		No

29. IF FEMALE, WAS THERE A PREGNANCY IN THE PAST 3 MONTHS? ☐ YES ☐ NO	30a. IF SURGERY IS MENTIONED IN PART I or II ENTER CONDITION FOR WHICH IT WAS PERFORMED.	30b. DATE OF SURGERY (Mo, Day, Year)

31. PROBABLE MANNER OF DEATH (Specify) Accident, suicide or homicide; or undetermined.	32a. DATE OF INJURY (Month, Day, Year)	32b. TIME OF INJURY	32c. INJURY AT WORK? (Yes or No)	32d. DESCRIBE HOW INJURY OCCURRED
		M		

32e. PLACE OF INJURY — At home, farm, street, factory, etc. (Specify)	32f. LOCATION (Street and Number or Rural Route Number, City or Town, State)

GENERAL INTERNATIONAL NON-DISCLOSURE AND NON-CIRCUMVENTION
AGREEMENT

General Business and Intermediary Services

Agreement number .... executed this th day of   1996 by and between
the parties mentioned in article 16.

Each individually and for the purpose of this Agreement considered to be independent
agents.
Nothing in this document is to be construed as a joint venture.
Neither Party is employed by the other party.
Neither Party is an authorised representative of the other Party.

WITNESSETH :

Whereas the Parties

are acting as Principals, Agents, Introducers or Brokers of international trade, and whereas
each Party wishes to assure the other Party that no Party to this agreement shall directly or
indirectly cause or knowingly allow the circumvention of any Party to this Agreement, it is
the expressed intent herein that each Party shall be entitled to and shall receive all monies
due to him or them under any agreement that may result from introductions by any Party to
this Agreement.   And now therefore for and in consideration of these and other mutual
covenants, agreements and promises contained herein, the Parties hereto agree as follows :

1. :   thus confirm that each of the named signatures separately and individually, their
        associates and companies for which they come, hereby agree that all companies,
        corporations, any/all divisions, subsidiaries, employees, agents, assignees,
        designees, consultants, partnerships, co-ventures, joint-ventures, trusts, sellers or
        buyers of prime bank guarantees or any other concern with which they are in any
        way concerned directly or indirectly and even occasionally, will not make any
        contact with, deal or otherwise enter into any transaction, directly or indirectly,
        with any Party to the Principal Agreements, already executed and yet to come, in
        respect to which this Non-Circumvention is made for, their agents, introducers,
        brokers, mandates, intermediaries, banking or lending institution, trust corporate
        or individual party1(s), lender(s), or borrower(s), party1(s), or party2(s)
        introduced by or by any other signatories, separately or individually and/or their
        associates of the introducing signatory(ies).

2 :   all parties agree hereby and guarantee not to circumvent on any or all of the parties
        to the agreement to a period of 7 (seven) years from the date affixed hereon by the
        last signature of execution, and is to be applied to the transactions entertained by
initials   first of three pages
        the parties, including subsequent follow-ups, repeat and extended or re-negotiated
        transactions, as well as to the initial transaction regardless of the initial transaction.

3 : in the event this stipulation is not adhered to, the circumvention is attempted or attained, the injured parties shall be entitled to a legal monetary penalty equal to the maximum compensation, or commissions, or fees, that the circumvented Party would have realised, monetary penalty that is at least equal to the commissions due following the Agreement in respect to which this Non-Circumvention agreement is made.

4 : any dispute that fails to do so, they shall submit the matter to the arbitration committee of International Chamber of Commerce Switzerland or Paris for settlement. Each party agrees hereby to bind itself to the ruling of the committee, judgement upon the award rendered by the arbitrator(s) may be entered in any court having jurisdiction thereof. Including the award of the aggrieved party/their heirs/assignees as a result of business conducted with the parties covered by this agreement, plus all court costs, attorney's fees and other charges and damages deemed fair by the arbitrator(s)

5 : The parties agree to keep completely confidential the names of any banks, lending institutions, corporation organisations, individuals or groups of individual lenders of borrowers, buyers or sellers introduced by any of the parties or their associates. Such identity shall remain confidential during the applicable transaction(s) and for the duration of this agreement, as shall any telephone numbers, addresses, telex numbers etc. Such information is considered the property of the introducing signatories, and the parties to this agreement hereby agree to discuss among themselves to determine as to what shall be disclosed and what procedure to use. Any controversy arising out of or relating to any part of this provision or breach thereof, which is not settled between the parties themselves, shall be settled by arbitration as designated in paragraph 4 above.

6 : The parties hereby shall not be held accountable for any failure to perform under the force majeure clauses as stated by the International Chamber of Commerce Paris, issue 500,which clauses are to be governed herewith

7 : The undersigned signatories of this agreement warrant that they have full personal and corporate legal authority vested in them personally by their corporation to enter into this agreement.
Each of the parties hereto warrants that there is no known violation of any law or any other rule they are due to respect by it in entering into this agreement.

8 : Notice of any and all notices required to be given by one party to another party shall be given by letter/fax and/or by registered mail and must be signed by the forwarder. Change of address must be given in writing.

initials   second of three pages

9 : Total agreement : this signed agreement shall constitute the only non-circumventi agreement between the parties hereto. No verbal representation,   warranties o statements by third parties and/or any trustees shall have any force   and affect whatsoev on this agreement. Any amendment to this agreement shall   be made in writing and sign

hereto and shall be witnessed and/or appended   hereto in the same fashion as   this
agreement.

10 :   The party1, party1's representative or party1's mandate must not circum-move for
        any payment

11 :   It is agreed that this contract shall be signed by all parties and they agree that this
        agreement will create and constitute an original, legal binding and enforceable
        document to any court of law

12 :   The parties hereto shall without any delay, this is at very latest before the start of
        the (first tranche of the) transaction, do all necessary to endorse and domiciliate
        this agreement in the bank(s) due to execute the principle contract;

        The same goes for the pay orders following the herein convened agreement.

13 :   It is agreed by the Parties hereto that this agreement may not be assigned,
        transferred, or in any manner gifted from the aforementioned Parties to any party
        or parties not named herein without the written consent or permission of all   Parties.

14 :   If any portion of this Agreement shall be declared void or unenforceable by any
        court,   arbitration committee, or administrative body or competent jurisdiction,
        such portion shall be deemed severable from the remainder of this Agreement
        which shall continue in all respects valid and enforceable. The Parties mutually
        agree to co-operate in any revision of this Agreement which may be necessary to
        meet the requirements of law.

15 :   The commission shall be as follows : **will be convened in separate payorder.**

16 :   The present contract is signed to be agreed on by the following persons :

FIRST PARTY   SECOND PARTY
NAME :   NAME :

for and on behalf of   for and on behalf of

SIGNATURE   SIGNATURE

DATE   DATE

JOINT VENTURE AGREEMENT

CONTRACT NUMBER 000/00/96

This agreement is entered into this _____th day of _____ 1996 by and between:

CFN Business Support Limited
Helios House, Gillsmans Hill, St Leonards on Sea, East Sussex, TN38 0SP England

who for the purpose of the joint venture created by this Agreement, is acting as "Managing Party", and who shall be hereinafter referred to as "JV-1". The place of business of this Joint Venture shall be at the address of "JV-1" as set forth above.

AND

_____

who for the purposes of the joint venture created by this Agreement, is acting as "Investing Party", and who shall be hereinafter referred to as "JV-2". Notwithstanding the above references to "JV-1" as Managing Party, and "JV-2" as Investing Party, both "JV-1" and "JV-2" shall be general partners of this joint venture.

WHEREAS the above are mutually desirous of transacting business in co-operation with one another for their mutual benefit.

WHEREAS "JV-1" has the ability to perform according to the terms and conditions of this agreement ; and

WHEREAS "JV-2" affirms that they are sophisticated investors who are duly authorised with full legal authority and have the financial capacity to enter into this agreement ;

NOW THEREFORE in consideration of the mutual covenants and agreements hereinafter set forth the parties hereto covenant and agree that the business of this agreement is to engage in a Secure Discretionary Trading Programme, hereinafter referred to as "The Programme", with "JV-1" acting as the Managing Party and "JV-2" acting as the Investing Party providing assets(s) for entry into "The Programme" under the terms and conditions as set forth hereinbelow :

(Initials)

(Initials)

I   TERMS

A.   TERM OF AGREEMENT :

The term of this Agreement shall be for four hundred (400) days, subject to renewal by mutual consent.

B.   TERMINATION OF AGREEMENT :

1. Termination of this Agreement shall be by mutual consent with thirty (30) days prior written notice and shall be sent by facsimile with the original sent immediately by registered letter or courier service to the parties whose signatures are affixed hereto. Immediately upon cancellation of this Agreement, the assignment of the asset(s) referenced in Paragraph II.A. hereinbelow, shall immediately revert to its rightful owners, Investing Party JV-2, without protest or delay, subject to normal clearing procedures which may be required by "The Program".

2. All other notices and other statements given or required in connection with this Agreement shall be made in writing and sent by facsimile with the original sent immediately by registered letter or courier service to the parties whose signatures are affixed hereto.

C.   DIVISION OF EARNINGS AND BANKING PROCEDURES :

1.   Program Returns, hereinafter "net earnings", on any and all ventures entered into by and on behalf of this Joint Venture shall be divided equally with fifty per cent (50%) of net earnings received by this Joint Venture Partnership from said Programmes and business ventures being paid to JV-1, and fifty per cent (50%) of net earnings from said Programmes and business ventures being paid to JV-2.

a.   Earnings shall be received via wire transfer to a bank designated by this Joint Venture according to the bank wiring instructions provided prior to the completion of trades; and,

b.   Managing Party, JV-1,shall make disbursements to JV-1 and JV-2 accor'ing to the division of profits outlined in Paragraph I.C.1. hereinbefore, with said disbursements being made via wire transfer to bank accounts designated by JV-1 and JV-2 according to the bank wiring instructions provided to the Managing Party prior to the completion of trades.

-------------------------   -------------------------
(Initials)   (Initials)

2. JV-1 shall cause an itemised accounting of all transactions and account activity to be maintained and copies of all transactions and account activity shall be immediately forwarded via facsimile to JV-2 with a quarterly itemised report provided to JV-2 within five (5) days, following the end of each calendar quarter.

3. LIMITED ACCESS TO TRADING/PROGRAM MANAGERS, PROGRAM BANK :

a. Investing Party, JV-2, hereby agrees that it shall not initiate or make any independent direct contact with the Trading Partner and/or Program Manager who is/are party to an agreement previously entered into by JV-1.

b. Investing Party, JV-2, hereby agrees that it shall not make any direct contact with the Program Bank, which, for the purposes of definition, will be the bank conducting the trading of bank instruments for The Program, nor will JV-2 contact any other banks involved with this series of transactions that are the subject of this Agreement.

c. Without limiting the generality of Clauses (a) and (b), Para I. Subparagraph C.3. hereinbefore, Managing Party, JV-1, agrees it shall provide an itemised accounting of any and all trading activity as outlined in Paragraph I.C.2. hereinbefore, and that JV-1 shall provide payment of earnings as outlined in Para. I.C.1.a.b.

II. RESPONSIBILITIES :

A. INVESTING PARTY JV-2 has agreed to provide various asset(s) for the purpose of generating a line/lines of credit / direct investment for entry into The Programme. However, the provision of any such assets shall not be construed as a capital contribution to the Joint Venture unless provided via wire transfer. JV-2 shall advise JV-1 of any prior encumbrances or hypothecation of the same subject asset(s).

B. MANAGING PARTY JV-1 agrees to manage this joint venture's participation in any of the Programmes as referenced hereinbefore, subject to review and consent by JV-2, and shall advise this Joint Venture of any known risks, or precautions recommended, and shall exercise its duties and responsibilities in good faith.

----------------------   ----------------------
(Initials)   (Initials)

C.   INVESTING PARTY JV-2 hereby authorises Managing Party JV-1 to enter
into and execute agreements on behalf of this Joint Venture Partnership in order to
facilitate the entry into a Trading Program, subject to the "good faith" policy in Para.
II.B. hereinbefore ;

D.   HOLD HARMLESS : However, without limiting the generality of Para.
II.A. and B. hereinbefore, if any action is taken against this Joint Venture,
individually or severally, as a result of actions taken or agreements entered into by
this Joint Venture, and any such actions are due to unforeseen circumstances or
circumstances beyond the control of this Joint Venture, each of the Parties shall
indemnify against and hold harmless the other Party from any damages or liability
resulting from said actions, unless Cause is shown, and for the purposes of this
Agreement, "Cause" shall mean an act or omission committed or omitted
fraudulently or in bad faith or which constitutes gross negligence.

E.   MANAGING PARTY JV-1 agrees to provide a full accounting of
transactions, advise in the event of any failure to perform on the part of The Program,
and make payments to JV-2 according to the division of profits as previously
outlined hereinbefore.

F.   MANAGING PARTY JV-1 shall retain the services of a professional
accountant to keep the books of the Joint Venture and to prepare an audited annual
report for each Party. Payment for such services shall be a Joint Venture expense.

G.   DEVOTION OF TIME : Managing Party JV-1 shall not be required to
devote full time to the affairs of the Joint Venture, but only that time reasonably
necessary to accomplish the purposes of the Joint Venture. The other Partners shall
not be required to devote any time to the Joint Venture, except such time as is
reasonably necessary to address Joint Venture issues.

H.   FAILURE TO PERFORM BY TRADING PROGRAMME : In the event of
the failure of any Secure Discretionary Trading Programme, or any other bank
instrument trading programme, to meet the minimum performance requirements in
any agreements entered into pursuant to this Agreement, it shall be the responsibility
of the Managing Party JV-1 to inform this joint venture of such failure, and upon
mutual consent, unilaterally withdraw from said agreement(s) and to demand release
of assignment of asset(s).

I.   LOANS TO THE JOINT VENTURE : Neither JV-1 nor JV-2 shall lend or
advance money to each other unless approved by all Partners.

III.   Both parties recognise the unique services rendered by their representatives (where
applicable) and agree that each shall be responsible for any commissions and/or fees
which have been agreed to in writing by that party as of the date of this Agreement.
The party which has incurred any such obligations shall indemnify and hold
harmless the other party against any claim, demand or expenses, however arising.

-------------------   --------------------
(Initials)   (Initials)
IV.   Each of the parties shall be responsible for their own institutional costs, and each
party, individually and separately, accepts liability for their respective taxes,

imposts, levies, duties or charges that may be applicable in the execution of their respective roles.

V.   This Agreement is subject to the non-circumvention and non-disclosure provisions of the relevant International Chamber of Commerce publication, latest revision, Paris, France, which shall remain in full force and effect for a period of five (5) years from the date hereof. This condition shall survive the termination of this Agreement for whatever reason.

VI.   Without limiting the generality of Paragraph V hereinafter, both parties hereby irrevocably agree not to circumvent, avoid, bypass, or obviate each other, directly or indirectly, avoid payment of fees or commissions in any transaction with any corporation, Joint Venture or individual, revealed by any party hereto to any other party or parties hereto, in connection with any loan, collateral, funding, commodity transaction, project or any other transaction of any type including any re-negotiations, renewal, extension, rollover, amendments, new contracts, agreements or third party assignments.

VII.   Without limiting the generality of Paragraphs V and VI hereinbefore, all parties hereby irrevocable agree not to disclose or otherwise reveal to any third party any confidential information provided by the other, particularly but not limited to that concerning Investing Partner's and Managing Partner's names, addresses, telephone numbers, fax numbers or other means of access thereto, nor bank information, code references, or any other such information advised to the other as being confidential or privileged without written consent of the party providing or making available such information.

VIII.   This Agreement is a binding agreement and shall be recognised by any court of competent jurisdiction as binding upon the parties hereto, their heirs, successors and assigns, agents, principals, attorneys and all associated parties involved in the transaction that is the subject matter of this Agreement.

IX.   This Agreement revokes, discharges and supersedes all prior representations, warranties or agreements between the parties concerning the subject matter of this Agreement except as specifically set forth herein.

X   If any portion of this Agreement is held by a court, tribunal or arbitrator of competent jurisdiction to be invalid, void or unenforceable, the remaining provisions of this Agreement will nevertheless continue in full force and effect, without being impaired or invalidated in any way.

-------------------------   -------------------------
(Initials)   (Initials)

XI.   On a timely basis a complete, properly executed, agreement shall be signed by all parties (2 originals). This Agreement may be executed in any number of counterparts, each of which shall be deemed original, but all of which taken together shall constitute one and the same document.

XII.   A signed copy of this Agreement shall have the same force and effect as the original.
        Copies shall include, but not be limited to, electronically-transmitted facsimiles, followed by hard copies containing "live" signatures.

XIII.   Both parties acknowledge that they have had adequate time and opportunity to consult with counsel of their own choosing prior to execution hereof, and have been fully informed as to their legal rights and obligations in connection herewith, and that having such advice, each has executed this Agreement freely and without reservation.

XIV.   All statements, commitments and representations under this Agreement are made by the respective party with full corporate and legal responsibility.

XV.   THE INVESTING PARTY, JV-2, HEREBY WARRANTS THAT ANY FUNDS OR ASSETS WHICH SHALL BE COMMITTED FOR THE ENTRY INTO A SDTP, OR EARNING ENHANCEMENT PROGRAM AS REFERENCED HEREINBEFORE SHALL BE GOOD AND CLEAN FUNDS OR ASSETS AND OF NON-CRIMINAL ORIGIN. BOTH JOINT VENTURE PARTIES HEREBY WARRANT THAT ANY FUNDS DERIVED FROM SUCH PROGRAMS WILL NOT BE USED FOR ANY ILLICIT OR TERRORISM PURPOSES.

XVI.   All disputes arising in connection with this Agreement shall be settled under the Rules of Conciliation and Arbitration promulgated by the International Chamber of Commerce by one (1) arbitrator appointed in accordance with said rules. The place of arbitration shall be Geneva in Switzerland and arbitration shall be carried out in the English language. Arbitration shall be binding on all parties, and any decision rendered in arbitration may be entered as a judgment in any court of competent jurisdiction.

XVII.   JV-1 reserves the right to assign this Agreement to a third party in order to facilitate entry into a Trading Program and provided all remaining obligations of JV-1 making such assignment, pursuant to this Agreement are performed in full by any such third party assignee, and so long as that assignment does not damage, dilute, or harm operation of any of the Programs or investments entered into by this Joint Venture.

-------------------------   -------------------------
      (Initials)   (Initials)

IN WITNESS WHEREOF the parties hereto have set their hands hereunder on the date adjacent to their respective signatures.

AGREED AND ACCEPTED :

"Managing Party", JV-1 :

--   ------------------------
                                                                            (date)

Stefan Groh
for and on behalf of
C.F.N. Business Support Limited

AGREED AND ACCEPTED :

"Investing Party", JV-2

--   ------------------------
                                                                            (date)

for and on behalf of

Index

French colonies 17
functional adaptation 59
functionalist school 4
functions 31

Galicia 5, 6, 7
Gambia 17
General Directorate of Linguistic
    Policy 7
generalization 61
Germany 5, 6, 7
gold certificate 26
good style 13
grades 92, 93, 94
grammatical person 60
Greece 7, 8
Guatemala 7

heads 63
Heres 5
hermeneutics 54
high-risk information 19, 114
Holland 7
honesty 11
Hong Kong 17
Hungary 6, 7

identification 13, 55
ideology 16
image 71
implicit brief 42
implicit information 99
improving 151, 75, 51, 102, 103, 104,
    105, 106
INCOTERMS 64
India 17
Indonesia 7
informant 18, 19
information types 32
informative function 31
initiator 10
Institute of Linguists 7
Institute of Translation and
    Interpreting 7
instrumental translation 54

insurance policy 43
interested parties 9, 11
internal reference function 31
International Federation of Translators
    (FIT) 5, 7, 8, 44, 118
internet 114
interpretation 12
intérprete jurado 6
intérprete público 6
interpreters 12
invoice 15, 37
involved party 9, 10
Iran 17
Iraq 7, 17
Ireland 4, 6, 7
Islamic law (*sharia*)17, 37
Israel 7
Italy 4, 6, 7

Japan 7, 17
job descriptions 90
joint-venture contract 26, 52, 87, 109,
    114, 122
Jordan 7
judges 12, 20
judicial authorities 7, 9
judicial body 9
judicial institutions 22
judicial sentence 28
judicial translators 12
Juntas Comerciales 7
jurisdiction 6
jurists 12

Kuwait 17

La Caixa 10, 50
Land 6
law enforcement officers 12
lawsuit 9
lawyers 11
layout 65
Lebanon 17
legal codes 113
legal norms 43